# I REMEMBER DYING

## WONDERFUL TRUE STORIES OF PEOPLE WHO RETURN FROM HEAVEN

# PAUL ROLAND

Foreword by Colin Wilson

**quantum**

LONDON • NEW YORK • TORONTO • SYDNEY

# quantum

An imprint of W. Foulsham & Co. Ltd
The Publishing House, Bennetts Close, Cippenham, Slough,
Berkshire, SL1 5AP, England

Foulsham books can be found in all good bookshops and direct from
www.foulsham.com

ISBN-13: 978-0-572-03264-7
ISBN-10: 0-572-03264-1

The exercises in this book are designed to improve self-awareness. They
should not be attempted while under the influence of alcohol or drugs of
any kind. Nor should they be practised by anyone in a psychologically
disturbed state of mind. Neither the editors of W. Foulsham & Co. Ltd
nor the author nor the publisher take responsibility for any possible
consequences from any treatment, procedure, test, exercise or action by
any person reading or following the information in this book.

Printed in Great Britain by Creative Print and Design (Wales), Ebbw Vale

# Contents

## Dedication

*This book is dedicated with love and appreciation to Sylvia Provins who led me to the first step on Jacob's Ladder.*

**Note:** All interviews were conducted by the author except where otherwise stated.

# Foreword by Colin Wilson

If I had to recommend one single work on the paranormal to someone who knew nothing about it, this is the book I would choose. No one can deny that Paul Roland is a complete master of his subject.

I have myself been writing about the subject for more than thirty-five years – since I produced in 1970 a book called *The Occult* – but I cannot match the author's one supreme qualification: that at the age of nine, has had a classic 'out-of-the-body experience', and has had several more since then.

Much of the latter part of the book contains interviews with people who had had 'near death experiences' – that is, apparently 'died', then came back. But the earlier part is a very comprehensive account of just about every aspect of the world of the paranormal.

The modern history of psychical research began in 1848, when in the small hamlet of Hydesville, New York State, the neighbours of the Fox family were asked to come into the house to hear a series of rapping noises, and one of them had the wit to ask the invisible rapper to answer questions in a code: one rap for yes, two for no. The entity told them that it was a peddlar who had been murdered for his money by the previous owner and buried in the cellar. (A skeleton was eventually found there.) The three young Fox sisters developed a remarkable ability to communicate with 'spirits' (such people became known as 'mediums'), and in no time at all, dozens of people all over America were able to do the same thing.

For this great flood of communication with 'the other side' I once coined the phrase 'the invasion of the spirit people'. And it has gone on without stopping ever since.

One serious problem soon became apparent: that fraudulent mediums found they could make a living at it, and were often caught faking. The scientists, who from the beginning had denounced 'spiritualism' as absurd superstition, lost no time in saying 'I told you so!'

In 1882, a number of serious-minded Victorians decided to try to get to the bottom of it, and founded a society for the scientific investigation of the paranormal, the Society for Psychical Research, whose members included Gladstone, Tennyson, Ruskin, Lewis Carroll and Mark Twain. Their investigations soon showed beyond all doubt that ghosts, poltergeists, telepathy and precognition of the future really took place. Yet they could never produce that ultimate piece of evidence that would convince the sceptics.

In this book, Paul Roland has described some of the most conclusive evidence ever, when a physician named Sir William Barrett began questioning nurses and doctors who had attended many death beds, and learned that, with great frequency, the dying saw visions of dead relatives who had apparently come to meet them – in some cases, relatives the dying person did not realise had 'passed over'. Barrett's *Death Bed Visions* should be studied by everyone who is interested in psychical research.

But it was not until November 1975 that an American doctor called Raymond A Moody produced a little paperback book called *Life After Life* that went on to sell millions of copies, and described some of the most stunning evidence so far – how hundreds of patients who had apparently died had been through a virtually identical experience, passing through a kind of tunnel, then emerging into some kind of realm beyond death. Many of them then realised that they had a choice – to go on into the blissful state of freedom from the body, or to return to earth. And many, including my own mother, made the return journey.

In the past few years, an even more astonishing advance has happened – what has become known as the EVP, or electronic voice phenomenon.

One June day in 1959, a Swedish birdwatcher named Friedrich Jurgenson was recording the voice of a chaffinch in his garden, and when he played it back, he was startled to hear his dead mother's voice calling out his pet name 'Friedel'. And soon he was recording the voices of many dead friends and relatives on tape by leaving the recorder switched on in an empty room. The voices were fragmentary and the messages brief, as if the communicators were having problems getting through.

Soon after, a Latvian psychologist named Konstantin Raudive read Jurgenson's book *Voices from Space*, and began his own experiments. He and Jurgensen began to collaborate, and when Raudive wrote a book called *Breakthrough*, the 'electronic voice phenomenon' became a sensation that was soon discussed all over the world. It looked as if the 'spirit people' were trying out a new method of communication.

It was in America that the great breakthrough came. George Meek, a businessman who had made his fortune from air-conditioning systems, decided to devote himself to studying psychic mysteries. When he heard about the electronic voice phenomenon, he set up a communication network of electronic experts all over the world.

One of these was a radio engineer named Bill O'Neil, who was also a gifted healer, and who had been trying to develop a radio device to help deaf mutes to 'hear'. And one day as he was tinkering with some unusual wavelengths, he was alarmed when he felt a hand on his shoulder, and turned to face a distinguished, well-dressed man who introduced himself as George Mueller, a professor who had worked for NASA, and had died in 1967. Now, he looked like a normal human being, and told O'Neil he was willing to help him construct a radio through which the dead could communicate direct with the living. He called it Spiricom.

For three years O'Neil and Professor Mueller worked on their invention. And on 22 September 1980, Mueller's voice suddenly came out of the radio, and O'Neil recorded their conversation. At last, a dead person was talking electronically to a living person.

Today, there are many scientists who believe that we are on the point of a completely new breakthrough in 'communication with the dead'. Whether this is so remains to be seen. But this is certainly something that should be borne in mind as you read the remarkable book that follows.

# Introduction

*Why should I fear? When was I less by dying?*

(Rumi)

This is not a typical book on the subject of life after death because for me that question was answered 40 years ago when, as a child, I had an out-of-body experience that altered my perception of reality. In fact, it was the first of many such experiences.

I can still recall waking from a dream to find myself soaring over the sea to 'visit' my grandmother and aunt in Ireland. I remember the sense of exhilaration of flying and the calmness with which I accepted that I was hovering over them as they sat watching TV, in the same room that I had played in whenever I visited them during the school holidays. After a few moments, having assured myself that they were fine, I snapped back into my body and woke with a jolt. There was no doubt about it. That was not a dream.

As I understand it, the experience had been triggered by a strong unconscious desire to see my aunt and grandma, combined with a latent ability to float free of my body – an ability that I believe we all share.

I have had OBEs, as they are commonly known, on several subsequent occasions and each time I have been fully conscious of being outside my body and in a state of heightened awareness quite distinct from the dream state. As an adult I would often wake from sleep to find myself in another part of the house, always with a feeling of intense relief and delight at being free from my physical shell. Unfortunately, the realisation was usually enough to pull me back into my body. However, one morning I awoke to find myself floating an inch or so above my body. I knew that if I opened my eyes I would return instantly to the physical, so I remained in that transient, disconnected state for some minutes, enjoying the sensation. I could have drifted off on another astral journey, but at the time I lacked the courage to let go and so I didn't take advantage of the opportunity. Each OBE has been a liberating sensation and one that appears to confirm that the astral, etheric, subtle or dream body is our natural state.

The survival of the soul is therefore, for me at least, not a question of faith but a fact. It is a natural phenomenon, not a supernatural one.

A number of recent surveys in the US and Europe have revealed that as many as one person in five claims to have had an out-of-body experience which they can recall in great detail. Unfortunately, many more dismiss their own episodes as a dream, either because they do not understand what they have experienced, or because the memory of it is muddied by subsequent dreams. Others may deny the evidence of their own senses because they have been conditioned by their religious or cultural upbringing to scorn all psychic and spiritual phenomena as irrational and unnatural. But whichever religion, philosophy or faith you subscribe to, OBEs and the closely related near-death experiences, are a universal phenomenon and the key to understanding our true nature.

At this point it may be useful to make a distinction between out-of-body experiences and near-death experiences. NDEs are similar to OBEs in that they involve the separation of the etheric body from the physical. But unlike OBEs, in which the individual wanders the physical world like a discarnate spirit prior to waking, an NDE involves the person passing through a tunnel of light to emerge in another, heavenly dimension, before returning to their physical body with a vivid recollection of the people and procedures used to revive them and, more significantly, with memories of the higher world. Unlike dreams, which can fade within moments, NDEs are always profound and life-transforming experiences that result in a renewed appetite for life.

So blissful and liberating is the experience that many are extremely reluctant to return to this world. One man berated the doctor who had resuscitated him by snapping, 'don't you ever do that again!'. The patient later apologised and explained his tetchiness by saying that he had felt that the doctor had effectively brought him back to a 'living death' when he could have had a 'real life'.

More and more people are now willing to admit to having had such experiences whereas 30 or 40 years ago they would have been reluctant to speak of such things for fear of being labelled delusional or even insane. Even now some physicians will not even entertain the idea that there might be more to human beings than flesh, blood and bones. The once devoutly sceptical Christian cardiologist Dr Michael Sabom of Atlanta, Georgia was recently berated by a colleague who questioned Sabom's new-found belief in out-of-body experiences. The contemptuous colleague claimed to have revived hundreds of patients, apparently bringing them back to life, not one of whom had ever mentioned having an OBE or anything like it. At that moment a man stood up behind the detractor, identified himself as a former patient of his, and added, 'I'm one of the people you saved – and I'll tell you right now, you're the last person I would ever tell about my near-death experience!'

The most incredible aspect of the phenomena is not that so many people from divergent backgrounds, beliefs and cultures have shared remarkably similar experiences, but that the die-hard sceptics continue to submit the same old arguments, at the same time denying the overwhelming experiential evidence.

Scientism, the belief that science has a monopoly on knowledge, is as dangerous as its opposite, creationism. Those of us who have had first-hand experience of psychic phenomena and spiritual experiences do not claim an exclusive insight into the nature and purpose of existence, for a near-death experience offers only a fleeting glimpse of a greater reality. As you will see from the personal accounts I have included, the ineffable magnitude of the divine remains a mystery even to those who have passed to the other side of life. The phenomena I describe in the following chapters are a fact of life, but their true significance is something we must each discover for ourselves.

# Psychic healing

The significance of the etheric double was demonstrated to me several years ago when I was suffering with chronic back pain. I couldn't stand or sit for more than a few minutes without having to shift my weight to alleviate the persistent ache in my lower back. I had treatment by both a chiropractor and an osteopath but neither offered more than just temporary relief.

Then one evening at the end of a meditation meeting the teacher announced that his spirit guides were telling him that someone in the room needed healing. He asked if everyone could remain seated to give their assistance. I was dumbstruck when he identified me as the prospective patient, but I was willing to try anything if it might help.

He then came over to me and placed one hand gently under my chin and another at the base of my spine. The others sat in silence with their hands on their knees, palms outwards, while visualising sending healing energy towards me. Whether or not they played a part I don't know, but within moments I felt a shift in what I can only describe as the core of my being and a sense of detachment as the teacher realigned my etheric body. When I opened my eyes I was aware once again of the density of my physical body but the pain had gone. It never returned.

Of course, the Chinese have known about the existence of the etheric double for centuries. It is the basis of their traditional holistic healing system, specifically acupuncture, in which needles are placed at key points along the body's meridian lines to release blockages of psychic energy. The Hindu and Buddhist traditions also acknowledge the existence of the subtle body which is linked to the physical at key points where the converging energy streams create whirling vortices known as 'chakras' (from the Sanskrit word meaning 'wheels'). And so-called psychic surgeons in Brazil and more recently in Europe and America have demonstrated the ability to psychically remove the source of dis-ease and dis-orders without anaesthetic in front of the television cameras. A detailed exploration of this phenomenon can be found in my book *Investigating The Unexplained*.

That said, the primary aim of this book is not to make yet another case for the existence of life after death (which should be self-evident from the wealth of experiential and scientific evidence), but to help you to awaken this higher self for guidance and insight into the greater reality.

Involuntary out-of-body experiences are often triggered by extreme exhaustion, serious illness, a violent shock or the effects of general anaesthetic. However, they can be induced at will. If you want to experience an OBE you will find several techniques to experiment with in the final section as well as exercises for projecting consciousness and testing the validity of other related phenomena.

Once you have experienced the exhilaration of floating free of your physical body and awakened to the heightened sense of awareness, which is quite distinct from the surreal nature of the dream state, you will intuitively know that our physical world is not the only reality.

*Because it is sometimes so unbelievable, the truth escapes becoming known.*
(Heraclitus, 500 BC)

11

# 1

# Belief in the Soul

*That which fashions the material form, develops, animates and cognises it,
must be something other than the form itself.*
(Swami Satprakashananda)

The belief that every individual has an immortal soul that survives
bodily death is common to almost every culture and civilisation in
recorded history. The idea that we all possess a spirit double that
leaves the body at the moment of death and possibly even during sleep is
a core feature of 57 cultures as diverse as the Azande in Africa, the Inuit of
Alaska and the Bacairis in South America, as well as being an underlying
principle of the major religions. Yet Western society considers itself too
sophisticated and worldly wise to accept what has been a central concept
of almost every culture since prehistoric times.

The reality of soul travel has inspired decorations in Etruscan temples,
and Egyptian pyramids, Native American and Inuit art and the paintings of
visionary Western artists such as Hieronymus Bosch, Gustave Doré,
William Blake, Henry Corbould and G.W. Russell.

While the universal belief in an immortal soul could be dismissed as
being no more than a primitive desire to deny our own mortality, such a
simple-minded explanation cannot account for the fact that many cultures
have shared the concept of three subtle bodies of increasing density, one
within the other; the equivalent to the astral body, spirit and soul of the
Western esoteric tradition. The Egyptians acknowledged the existence of
the ka, the ba and the akh (which gave rise to the practice of placing
mummies in three sarcophagi of increasing refinement); the Greeks
considered the significance of the psyche, the pneuma and the nous; the
Muslims talked of the sirr, ruh and nafs; the Hindus of the atman, jiva and
pranamayakosha; while the Jewish mystics contemplate the nature of the
neshamah, the ruah and the nefash.

In Europe the belief in a spirit double capable of leaving the body at
night gave birth to the Greek eidolon, the Roman larva, the German
doppelganger, the English fetch, the Norwegian vardger and the Scottish

taslach, all of which feature in their country's folklore under various names reflecting regional variations and dialects. The same theme surfaces in symbolic form in the Celtic, Greek and Nordic myths in which heroes venture into the underworld to rescue the souls of their loved ones.

Later writers and poets, including Goethe, Dickens, Tennyson, Emily Brontë, D.H. Lawrence, Virginia Woolf, Ernest Hemingway, Jack London and Aldous Huxley are known to have drawn on their own out-of-body experiences for inspiration. The French author de Maupassant, for example, would casually refer to the fact that his double appeared in his study when he was deep in thought, while the poet Percy Bysshe Shelley is said to have been amused when informed that his astral twin had been observed, several miles away, by his friends, among them his literary rival, Lord Byron. However, on the one occasion when Shelley caught sight of his own double it proved to be a prophecy of his own death. The doppelganger was pointing out to sea indicating the place where the poet later drowned in a boating accident.

It is thought that artists, poets and writers are natural psychics, their highly developed imagination enabling them to visualise scenes in a temporary dreamlike reality prior to bringing them into being. We all share this facility to bring our desires into being. It is the basis of self-help programmes and ritual magic, but most of us fail to understand its significance and so fritter it away in idle daydreaming.

## Shamanic soul travel

The ritual practice of soul travel or astral projection, as it is known in the esoteric tradition, is still central to the tribal societies of Africa, Australasia, North and South America and the Arctic, where shamans are entrusted with healing, appeasing the nature spirits and escorting the dead to the netherworld. With a combination of ritual drumming, dancing, chanting, fasting and natural narcotics they induce a state of ecstasy (the word's original meaning is 'to stand outside') allowing them to leave their bodies and commune with their spirit guides, animals and their ancestors. Some remain outside their bodies for days interceding with the spirits on behalf of their community or searching for lost animals, which are often the tribes' only asset.

In the East, soul travel was traditionally a spiritual discipline promising enlightenment and thereby liberation from the cycle of death and rebirth. The ancient Chinese practised a form of meditation which taught the initiate how to concentrate their inner essence (the thankhi) through breath control, posture and contemplation. A manual detailing the techniques required for mastering this technique, *The Secret Of The Golden Flower*, demanded rigorous self-discipline and a willingness to subjugate the self in order to liberate the spirit body through the 'pineal door', often known as the 'third eye'.

It is believed that the ancient Egyptians practised similar disciplines and that the empty sarcophagus in the King's Chamber of the Great Pyramid at Giza was reserved for initiation rites in which the acolyte would lie in preparation for projecting his astral body to the stars. In the 1930s the occult scholar Dr Paul Brunton took the opportunity to test the theory and found himself 'drawn, ghost-like' out of his body against his will. The cobra (symbol of wisdom) which crowns every pharaoh's headpiece represented the pineal doorway through which the spirit could exit.

The Buddhists practise similar techniques in the hope of liberating the rupa while the Hindu yogis devote themselves to awakening kundulini (the sleeping serpent) which rises from the base chakra to strike the brow chakra, releasing the true self. In the Western esoteric tradition initiates visualise travelling the 22 paths on the Kabbalistic tree of life, in an inner exploration of the symbolic landscape of the psyche known as pathworking. The paths link ten spheres which are visualised as inner temples, each representing specific qualities to be acquired by the initiate.

## The true philosophers

The ancient Greeks considered it both prudent and practical to contemplate what might greet them on the other side of life and so formed secret societies to initiate their fellow philosophers into what they called the 'mysteries'. In fact, the term 'philosopher' denotes one who contemplates 'the things under the earth', by which they meant 'beyond death'.

It is clear from the following passage in Plato's *Phaedra* that Hades could be either heaven or hell depending how prepared one was for the afterlife.

> *It looks as if those also who established rites of initiation for us were no fools, but that there is a hidden meaning in their teaching when it says that whoever arrives uninitiated in Hades will lie in mud, but the purified and initiated will dwell with gods. For there are in truth, as those who understand the mysteries say, many who bear the wand, but few who become bakchoi [devotees]. And these latter are in my opinion no other than those who have given their lives to true philosophy.*

14

The reference to mud appears to be symbolic of the slow progress made by the uninitiated and not a literal torment. It is my understanding that all references to the torments of purgatory and hell are purely allegorical or symbolic of disturbed states of mind.

Plato wrote one of the earliest recorded accounts of an NDE in Western literature, the story of Er, a fallen soldier whose voyage through the underworld was an attempt to introduce the concept into Greek national consciousness.

As the Argentinian writer Jorge Luis Borges observed two thousand years later, 'The Platonists sense intuitively that ideas are realities.'

In the first century AD the Greek biographer Plutarch recorded the allegedly true experience of Aridaeus of Asia Minor who left his body after receiving a blow on the head. While wandering confused in the space between the worlds, Aridaeus met his deceased uncle who reassured him that he was still alive and should return to his body without further delay. In this same essay Plutarch refers to the limitations of the 'silver cord' which prevent Aridaeus from venturing further into the afterlife. 'Your soul's cable is stretched down to your body, to which it is anchored, and allows no further upward slack or play.' The implication is that Aridaeus is still bound to the body. It is not his time to leave the world.

Hermotimus, a Greek philosopher and mystic of the sixth century BC, was not so fortunate. He was an inveterate astral traveller and in the habit of regaling his wife with tales of foreign shores. Eventually she tired of this and resolved to teach him a lesson. She approached two of his friends and asked them to remove her husband's body to another location so that he would only find it after a long search and hopefully be less inclined in future to leave her for such long periods. Unbeknown to her, the pair were in fact his rivals and they took the opportunity to cremate their enemy as soon as he vacated his body. When Hermotimus returned in spirit to find his body reduced to ashes he haunted his wife until it was her turn to join him in the spirit world.

# 2

# The Soul and the Scriptures

Near-death experiences are generally and mistakenly considered to be a modern phenomenon, one which only came to public notice in the 1970s through the publication of best-selling studies by Raymond Moody, Elizabeth Kubler-Ross and their successors.

But both OBEs and NDEs are a recurring feature in the sacred literature of all the major world religions, faiths and philosophies, as is the description of a celestial paradise which is said to be the ultimate destiny of each deserving soul. Christianity was founded on the belief that Jesus rose from the tomb and was seen 'in the spirit', while Islam honours the Night Journey of the prophet Mohammed, which is an allusion to soul travel, and Jewish mystics attained personal experience of the divine through visualisations that are still practised to this day. If heaven was a mere myth, an empty promise to give comfort to the weary or a reward for the righteous, it would not be such a significant feature of the Jewish Torah, the Christian Bible, the Islamic Koran, nor the sacred Hindu and Buddhist texts.

Blind faith alone cannot sustain a human being through the trials of life. There has to be an intuitive sense that what we have been told awaits us in the afterlife is, in essence at least, true. As Dr Carol Zaleski of Harvard University has noted, 'A conviction that life surpasses death, however intensely felt, will eventually lose its vitality and become a mere fossil record, as alien as any borrowed doctrine, unless it is tested and rediscovered in daily life.'

It is my contention that it has been and continues to be rediscovered by an increasing number of 'ordinary people' in every country and culture around the world each and every day. Of course, there are many people who are equally convinced that there is no afterlife and that when they die they cease to exist. Such convictions serve to prove the power of the ordinary mind, or ego, which rationalises its existence by denying a greater reality.

16

Even if we have no conscious memory of the heavenly realm, our higher or true self does. In fact, it is still connected to this higher dimension of being, a belief alluded to by Jesus of Nazareth when he encouraged his followers to seek 'the kingdom of heaven within'. Similarly it is the 'Buddha within' whom the Buddhists acknowledge when they bow before a likeness of their founder, for theirs is a philosophy of awakening and not worship.

But often the revelation of this great reality is wilfully obscured in the sacred texts by symbolism, either to preserve the mystery of altered states of awareness for its initiates or because those who recorded it did not understand the true nature or significance of the experience.

## Death and the end of days

Death is an alien concept to the Eastern religions, which are founded on the belief that nothing dies, in the sense that it ceases to exist. All life forms are animated by universal energy and energy cannot die. It can only be transformed.

Similarly, while the physical form of a human being may cease to function and disintegrate after death, the personality lives on in a non-physical reality until it is reborn in a new body.

For this reason there is no 'final judgement' in the Eastern philosophies nor physical resurrection at the 'end of days' (hence the Hindu custom of cremation and the Tibetan tradition of feeding the deceased to animals instead of burying them). In its place there is the belief in a continual cycle of death and rebirth from which we are required to attain both insight and experience.

Both Hinduism and Buddhism are concerned solely with the spiritual evolution of the individual and not with the fate of humanity as a whole. This is the fundamental difference between the Eastern philosophies and the orthodox Western religions, which place great emphasis on the will of God and the expunging of original sin – concepts that are alien to the East.

## Hinduism

In Hinduism there are a limitless number of worlds and heaven is just one stage on the journey back to the source, not the ultimate destination of the soul. In this it has much in common with Buddhism and Judaism, but also with early Christianity, which appropriated the concept of seven heavens from the Jewish mystics.

According to Hindu mythology, paradise is a 'kingdom of inexhaustible light' (*Riga Veda* IX 113:7), a dreamlike dimension, an alternative reality, no less real than our own world but one requiring a heightened state of awareness, which is alluded to in the *Brhadaranyaka Upanishad* by the phrase, 'by the mind alone is it to be perceived' (4.4.19).

Such imagery invites comparison with the descriptions of heaven given by those who have experienced the NDE phenomenon. To attain this state of bliss the authors of the *Rig Veda* urge Hindus to abstain from the pleasures of the physical world so that they might see the divine in all things and perceive the unity of existence. At this level of awareness they will become a Brahmana (knower of Brahman) and upon death attain moksha (release) so as to merge with the supreme soul.

The *Brhadaranyaka Upanishad* (which serves as a commentary on the Vedas) compares the individual soul to a lump of salt that is drawn from the sea and must ultimately return to the source:

> All the diverse elements, in the end, go back to the soul and are absorbed in it, as all waters are finally absorbed in the ocean... A lump of salt may be produced by separating it from the water of the ocean. But when it is dropped into the ocean, it becomes one with the ocean and cannot be separated again.

The legend of Usha who journeyed to exotic foreign lands in her dreams is just one of the many references to the immortality of the soul and the possibility of soul travel in the Hindu *Bhagavata Purana*, a sacred text written in the tenth century.

Jainism shares the Hindu belief in the transmigration of souls, which it calls the jina, or 'victor'.

On a superficial level the various strands of Hinduism appear to contradict each other, but closer study reveals that they are simply different facets of the same philosophy.

Sankhya Hinduism is atheistic in the sense that it denies the existence of an omnipotent God and views the physical world and the heavenly dimension as separate realities.

The Yoga tradition makes the same distinction between the worlds of spirit and matter, but subscribes to a belief in a universal creator, Brahman.

The three branches of the Vedanta sect offer variations on the idea that the physical universe is a manifestation of Brahman's divine will. Suffering is therefore a result of our denial of our divine nature, which can only be ended when we awaken to the idea that we are 'sparks of the divine fire' with the ability to create our own heaven and hell in both this dimension and the next.

Such beliefs are central to the philosophies of self-knowledge such as Buddhism and Kabbalah (the esoteric aspect of Judaism), but incompatible with the orthodox religions of faith in which followers delegate responsibility for their spiritual development to a messianic saviour.

Perhaps more revealing is the reference in the *Rig Veda* (one of Hinduism's most ancient texts) to the acquisition of 'another body' (the atman or soul) which serves as a vehicle for journeying through the world of spirit.

Whilst it is perhaps inevitable that various sects of the same religion will envisage the creator according to their own hopes and fears, it is significant that all branches of Hinduism share an understanding of the core concepts of karma (the universal law of cause and effect) and samsara (reincarnation). The nature and will of the divine must inevitably be a matter of speculation, in Hinduism as in all religions, whereas the natural processes of life, death and rebirth can be determined, to a degree, through individual spiritual experience and by observing how universal laws manifest in the physical dimension.

# Buddhism

*If you want to know your past life, look into your present condition; if you want to know your future life, look at your present actions.*

(Tibetan Buddhist teaching)

Buddhism, which began as a reform movement within Hinduism, shares the Hindu belief in both karma and reincarnation, the endless cycle of death and rebirth from which the only escape is through enlightenment or self-realisation. The ultimate aim is the total absorption of the individual within the universal consciousness from which it came.

But whereas Hinduism is a reservoir of wisdom, myth, speculation and superstition from diverse sources compiled over many centuries, Buddhism is rooted in the teachings of one man, its founder Gautama Buddha (meaning 'awakened one'). Nevertheless, the various schools of Buddhism are committed to honouring their own interpretation of their founder's insights into the nature of existence and offer differing methods for attaining nirvana ('bliss').

Curiously, Buddhists do not believe that each individual possesses a soul in the Judaeo-Christian sense, but that it is instead comprised of five elements: a physical body, emotions, the senses, will-power and consciousness. Together these elements constitute the personality, which dissolves upon death leaving only pure consciousness (rupa) to inhabit a new body or ascend to the higher states of being. From here it can guide the lives of those on earth in the form of a boddhisattva (one who aspires to be a Buddha).

A distinction is made between the lower self, (the ordinary mind or ego) and the higher self (or super ego). By consciously subjecting the lower self to the greater will of the higher self we can awaken the Buddha within and begin the process leading to enlightenment. Such a process is not to be considered as a struggle or suppression of our worldly self, but a reconciliation of these two complementary aspects of our psyche which is intended to cultivate a compassionate detachment from the material world so that we become 'in the world but not of it'.

Considering that Buddhism is a philosophy centred on compassion and peace of mind, it is unsettling to read the graphic descriptions of hell in their sacred texts. But modern Buddhists consider these to be symbolic of a state of mind. Of more significance are the Buddhist descriptions of heaven as varying states of awareness. These recall the seven heavens of Jewish mysticism and the early Christian concept of a multidimensional heavenly kingdom to which Jesus is thought to have alluded when he said, 'In my Father's house are many mansions.'

Entrance to paradise is dependent upon the accumulation of a person's karma and when this credit is spent the soul must return to earth to take possession of a new body. The main theme of the Buddhist belief system is transience. Everything, even the peace of paradise, is temporary. The only hope of release from the cycle of suffering (death and rebirth) is the complete surrender of the self in order to become one with the source.

## The Tibetan delok

The Tibetans have a special term for those who have passed into the bardo (the transitional state between life and death) and returned to tell of their experience. They are called the delok and the process they describe has direct parallels to the NDE phenomena.

Sogyal Rinpoche, author of *The Tibetan Book of Living and Dying* (1993) tells of the sixteenth-century mystic Lingza Chokyi who spent her life trying to convince others of the truth of what she had experienced. Chokyi was in the throes of a critical illness when she left her body and looked back on it with some disgust. She likened it to a pig's corpse wearing her clothes. For some time she remained among her family but became increasingly frustrated when they refused to acknowledge her presence, or set a place for her at the dinner table. Eventually she was drawn away from her home by a voice, which she suspected was that of her deceased father, into a new, alternative reality. She describes this place as a country where she met other wandering spirits and was greeted by a divine being who ordered her to return to life because it was not yet her time to die.

In the Tibetan Buddhist teachings, near-death experiences are not an altered state of consciousness, but simply a state of heightened awareness in which the mind is free to wander through various realms interpreting what it sees according to its expectations. If it sees something it cannot understand it may return to the body with the impression that there is something to fear. Negative NDEs – which incidentally are extremely rare – may therefore be nothing more than the individual's inability to cope with an unfamiliar sensation or state of mind. Those who fear what might lie beyond the tunnel of light, for example, or who are disorientated on finding themselves free of their bodies and suspended in space may panic and return convinced that they had narrowly escaped being sucked into a dark pit. Such experiences may be the origin of the concept of hell. Similarly, those who are not aware that they are discarnate may find themselves in a place where like-minded individuals are wandering aimlessly, and when they finally realise where they are they may also return in fear with images of soulless, zombie-like creatures.

## The Tibetan Book of the Dead

*The hour has come to part with this body, composed of flesh and blood;*
*may I know the body to be impermanent and illusory.*

Not all sacred texts are allegorical. The *Tibetan Book of the Dead* is a handbook for the departing soul giving explicit instructions for easing the passing from this life to the next. It was intended to be read aloud by those who watched over the dead on 49 successive days – being the period the soul is believed to linger in the bardo, the intermediate state between death and rebirth.

Though it was written more than a thousand years ago, its description of the three phases of death is strikingly similar to modern accounts of NDEs, although there is no mention of a celestial paradise because the Tibetans believe that the bardo is a state of mind in which the discarnate consciousness creates its environment according to its expectations.

The first stage, called chikai bardo, occurs when consciousness is suspended at the point of separation from the physical body. At this moment the individual is unaware that they are dead. Only when they look down on their own lifeless body do they realise that this ethereal essence is their true self:

*Thine intellect hath been separated from thy body.*
*Because of this inability to loiter, thou oft-times wilt feel*
*perturbed and vexed and panic-stricken...*

21

There follows a detailed description of the etheric body and its capabilities:

> Having a body [seemingly] fleshly [resembling] the former [the physical body] and that to be produced, endowed with all sense faculties and power of unimpeded motion.

During the dissolution or casting-off of the body, the discarnate personality may be subjected to hallucinations that invite comparison with the tunnel of light described in NDEs.

The reading of the relevant passages is intended to familiarise the recently deceased with their new reality for as in NDEs they can still hear and see the living, even though they themselves cannot be seen or heard.

The next stage is crucial if the spirit is to be free to enter the 'clear, primordial light' of the higher world. The following passages stress the importance of letting go of all emotional attachments to people and places so that the soul may ascend into the light.

But some may be unwilling to or unable to relinquish their possessions or may harbour regrets or resentment that will effectively bind them to the earth plane. Others may be literally haunted by their own evil deeds and they will only exorcise these memories by re-living them in a succession of hells of their own making.

Once they have severed all detachments they are judged by their own conscience, a process that finds an echo in many cultures down the centuries:

> ... the Good Genius, who was born simultaneously with thee, will come now and count out thy good deeds [with] white pebbles, and the Evil Genius, who was born simultaneously with thee, will come now and count out thy evil deeds [with] black pebbles...Then the Lord of Death will say, 'I will consult the mirror of karma'. So saying, he will look in the mirror, wherein every good and evil act is vividly reflected.

The 'lords of death' are personifications of the individual's inner demons, 'thine own hallucinations', a concept which predates Jung's archetypes by a millennium.

> O now, when the bardo of reality upon me is dawning!
> Abandoning all awe, fear, and terror of all phenomena,
> May I recognise whatever appears as being my own thought forms,
> May I know them to be apparitions in the intermediate state.

Having faced the consequences of his actions he can then submit to the mercy of the Buddha within, his own divine essence who determines whether he can enter nirvana or must reincarnate. Assuming that most souls will need to return to the world for further trials, the concluding prayers are intended to guide it to re-enter under the most favourable circumstances:

> *O now, when the bardo of taking rebirth upon me is*
> *dawning!*
> *One-pointedly holding fast to a single wish,*
> *May I be able to continue the course of good deeds*
> *through repeated efforts;*
> *May the womb-door be closed, and the revulsion*
> *recollected.*

According to the Tibetan masters, it does not matter whether the spirit was a Buddhist because we will all share the same experience of the peaceful and wrathful deities.

However if we are familiar with the imagery we will understand the nature of the experience and not be unduly disturbed.

> *O procrastinating one, who thinks not of the coming of*
> *death,*
> *Devoting yourself to the useless doings of this life,*
> *Improvident are you in dissipating your great*
> *opportunity;*
> *Mistaken, indeed, will your purpose be now if you*
> *return empty-handed from this life.*

> (*Tibetan Book of The Dead.* Evans-Wentz translation)

# Islam

Islam was founded in the sixth century AD by the prophet Mohammed, who preached a monotheistic faith in the Judaeo-Christian tradition. Under his leadership the Muslims (meaning 'those who submit to God's will') defeated their enemies and established a civilisation far in advance of that which existed in Europe at the time.

Islam places great emphasis on the afterlife as a paradise for the faithful and which it describes in terms that were clearly designed to appeal to a nomadic desert people. The gardens of paradise (al-Jannah) are lush and sustained by running streams of crystal clear water, milk and honey. Being a patriarchal society, Islam promises a multitude of lusty willing maidens for righteous males, but no mention is made of the reward awaiting virtuous women. The garden is a veritable Aladdin's cave of precious stones in which all wishes are granted and this is perhaps the key to the Islamic paradise. Al-Jannah will be whatever you want it to be, a place where old men become young again and where even the least deserving are serviced by 72 women and 80,000 slaves. Hell, on the other hand, is for the infidel and the idolater, a place of flesh-eating fire and ceaseless attacks by serpents and scorpions.

# Judaism

One of the earliest recorded episodes of astral travel occurs in the Old Testament. In the second Book of Kings the prophet Elisha prefigured our modern psychic spies when he practised a form of remote viewing to forewarn the Israelites of impending attack by the Syrian armies. Every time the Syrian king manoeuvred his troops into position he found himself facing the Israelites who were entrenched behind newly erected defences. The origin of the umbilical 'silver cord' connecting the etheric body to its physical counterpart can also be traced back to the Old Testament: Ecclesiastes (12:6) refers to the severing of a silver cord releasing the soul back to God.

There are fleeting references to heaven and hell in the Torah, the Hebrew Bible, but no explicit mention of an immortal soul. There are descriptions of a dark pit called Sheol into which the righteous and wicked alike descend to wait upon the will of God, but it is not a place of devils and torment. It is an all-consuming darkness, a place of forgetfulness, silence and sleep. In contrast, heaven is the abode of God alone.

Such nihilistic beliefs are thought to have been an expression of the Jews' disillusionment and despair which came about as a consequence of their repeated enslavement. These beliefs were later tempered by the hope that a Messiah would come to their aid and rid them of their enemies. As a result, later texts placed less emphasis on Sheol and offered the promise of heaven as an eternal land of milk and honey for those who led righteous lives.

But as with the other major religions, Jewish orthodox practices and scripture reflect only one aspect of the tradition. Encoded in the rituals and sacred texts there are hidden (esoteric) teachings that reveal the true significance of existence and the nature of the universe. For centuries these secret teachings were passed on from rabbi to pupil by word of mouth because they feared that if they were written down they might fall into the hands of the profane. For this reason the teachings were given the name Kabbalah (meaning 'to receive'). Once an initiate knows how to interpret the symbolic language of the Torah, the Old Testament stories are revealed to be much more than a history of the Jewish people. Instead they are read as a metaphor for our journey through life.

Kabbalah is the ancient Jewish metaphysical philosophy which seeks to explain our place and purpose in existence through a symbolic diagram known as the tree of life, on which are arranged the divine attributes of the creator (see diagram 1). These complementary qualities are also manifest in finite form in every human being, although culture and conditioning encourage us to emphasise some at the expense of others. But by becoming conscious of these characteristics and bringing them into balance we can become fully realised and enlightened beings. It is this central concept, emphasising the leading of initiates to self-realisation or enlightenment, that Kabbalah shares with the Eastern philosophies.

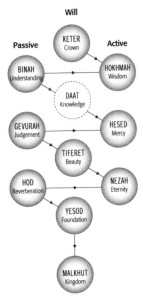

*Diagram 1: Path of the Lightning Bolt*

# Kabbalah – 'as above, so below'

According to Kabbalistic tradition the universe came into being because God wished to know Himself, to express His love in the act of creation and to experience what He had created. To do so the endless light of the absolute all (en sof), emerged from the darkness of the absolute nothing (ayin) in the form of a lightning bolt (en sof aur) and was refracted as through a prism at ten different levels, symbolised by the sephiroth or spheres, before grounding itself in form and matter (see diagram 2).

What was once pure consciousness had condensed into a composite entity. For this reason every atom and element in the universe is seen as an expression of the divine.

The descent of the divine from spirit into matter is envisaged in terms of four distinct stages of creation, as four interdependent and interpenetrating worlds, each containing the essence of those from which it was generated (see diagram 2). These are the worlds of emanation (the realm of spirit or divine essence), creation (the dimension of universal consciousness), formation (the astral, emotional or dream world) and action (our physical world).

The world of emanation (azilut) is the realm beyond time and space where the laws and dynamics of creation await the divine will.

The world of creation (beriah), is inhabited by the archangels, each personifying the quality and energy of a specific sephirah.

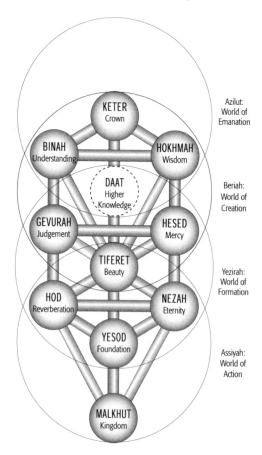

*Diagram 2: The Four Worlds*

The third world is the world of formation (yezirah), which psychics call the astral plane, which we wander through in our more lucid dreams and to which we return during the first stage of the transition we call death. It is the dimension where our thoughts take on temporary form, where we create our own personal heaven or hell. It is the realm described in the Old Testament as the Garden of Eden where the 'models' for the various species were determined before incarnating in their infinite variety in the fourth world, (asiyyah) the world of action.

As an embodiment of the divine we exist in the four worlds simultaneously, because we possess a spirit, an intellect, an emotional body and a physical form.

## The mysteries of life, death and rebirth

Science has revealed the physical processes of ageing, disease, death and decay which were considered a sacred mystery only a few hundred years ago. Science has also identified the biological stages of conception, gestation and birth to the point where we should soon be able to create life artificially by cloning a human being. But it remains for those who have personally experienced out-of-body awareness to reveal what actually happens at the moment of death and in the realm between lives.

Their accounts confirm that death is not an end, merely a transformation from one state of awareness to another; a casting off of the fragile shell we call our body. But the majority of these individuals are 'ordinary people' who feel unable to put their impressions in context, while the mystics frequently express their visions in obscure symbolism relevant to the religious and cultural conditioning of their time, thus leaving us none the wiser.

As a result, the process of dying and transition remains couched in vague, subjective or fanciful imagery with no sense of where this heavenly realm might be or where it figures in the greater scheme. There are detailed descriptions of the post-mortem state in the literature of the esoteric traditions, but even the Buddhist *Tibetan Book of The Dead*, which describes the first stages of death, does not offer a structural scheme of human existence.

To my knowledge only Kabbalah offers a working model of the universe in which the higher worlds are envisaged as being a more refined expression of our material dimension. In such a consistent and logical scheme all spiritual and psychic experiences are seen as offering glimpses of a greater reality, rather than as random phenomena.

# What happens at the moment of death?

According to Kabbalistic tradition, each of us came into being upon separation from the source, acquiring bodies of increasing density during our descent into matter.

We are therefore comprised of four elements: a physical body, a psyche, a vital soul and the divine spark of pure consciousness, each of which exists in its own sphere of influence, in one of the four interpenetrating realities known collectively as Jacob's Ladder (see diagram 3). We alone among earth's creatures are able to focus exclusively on our physical needs or express a whole gamut of emotions from sentimentality to rage. We can intellectualise, rationalise, reflect, recall or aspire to fulfil our potential and we also have the unique capacity to heighten our awareness from these lower levels to the spiritual whenever we pray, meditate or use our imagination, which is the key to higher consciousness. In this sense we operate in the realms of spirit (azilut), thought (beriah),

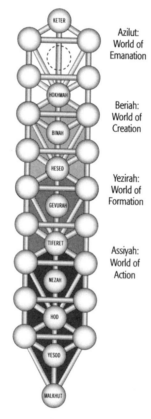

Azilut:
World of
Emanation

Beriah:
World of
Creation

Yezirah:
World of
Formation

Assiyah:
World of
Action

*Diagram 3: The Four Worlds as Jacob's Ladder*

emotion (yezirah) and action (assiyah) simultaneously and unconsciously. But the more self-aware we become, the more control we will be able to exercise over our body, our emotions, our thoughts and our connection with our higher self.

In this context OBEs can be seen as involving a temporary detachment between the physical body (assyatic) and the psyche (yeziratic), whereas death involves the permanent separation of these two vehicles.

In the Kabbalistic scheme heaven is not our ultimate destination, but only the first stage on our progression back to the source which is likely to take many lifetimes. The celestial garden described in numerous NDEs is the next dimension to our own, yezirah. This is the world of illusions where our liberated psyche, previously dulled by the limitations of the five physical senses, is now overwhelmed by the intensity of the energy at this heightened state of awareness, which accounts for the sense of bliss and the luminosity of the colours experienced at this level.

Death occurs when the vital soul (nefesh) can no longer hold the physical body and its etheric double, the psyche, in synchronisation. This may be due to prolonged illness which weakens an individual's hold on life or from a violent act which wrenches the two apart. At this point the umbilical silver cord of etheric energy linking the psyche to the body becomes detached, mirroring the birth process, at the point where the centre of consciousness corresponding to knowledge of the body (daat) was joined to the lower self or ego centre (yesod) on the psyche (see diagram 4). This silver cord is a feature of many OBEs.

So strong is the empathic link between the two elements that it is not uncommon for the psyche to remain within the vicinity of the body for several days, which would explain the many sightings of the deceased at their own funeral. In the Jewish tradition this apparition is known as the zelim, or shadow image, but it is common to all cultures, hence the universal custom of ritual farewells to ease its passing into the world beyond. Our ancestors knew the importance of severing attachments for the sake of both the living and the dead.

Those souls who are not able or willing to ascend to the next level, because of attachments, addictions or their determination to resolve unfinished business, remain earthbound as ghosts. Others may simply be unaware that they are dead either because they could not conceive of a life after death, or because they were unprepared. Until they are made aware of the fact that they no longer have an impact on the physical world they may habitually re-live their daily routines.

Those few souls who experience the symbolic state we call purgatory are bringing this state into being in a form that conforms to their beliefs so that they can indulge their need to castigate themselves for their actions on earth. It is significant and revealing that purgatory is traditionally envisaged in terms of the four elements (boiling mud, ice, fire, lack of water etc.) as this illusion is generated by the forces operating in the 'pit' of the yeziratic world, or if we put it in psychological terms, in the egocentric region of the psyche.

But the majority of us will recuperate from life's trials at the centre of the yeziratic world, in the heavenly Eden, while more advanced souls will ascend to the realm of pure spirit (beriah). Only these highly developed souls can choose the time of their next incarnation, because only they are self-aware and know what tasks they need to accomplish and what experiences they require to attain self-realisation.

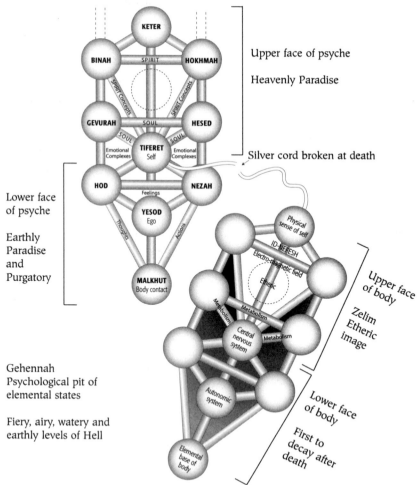

*Diagram 4: The separation of the psyche and the physical body at death (with acknowledgement to Z'ev ben Simon Halevi)*

# Christianity

The New Testament makes no mention of what becomes of individual souls after death, but instead places great emphasis on the ultimate destiny of human kind at the end of days. This is in striking contrast to the wisdom teachings found in the Gospel of Thomas, which is said to contain the original, uncensored sayings of Jesus. In this heretical text, which the Church has sought to suppress, Jesus speaks of the Kingdom of Heaven as being within each and every one of us. No one can be denied access to this sacred space and we exclude ourselves only by believing that, as poor miserable sinners, we need to obtain someone else's permission to enter. And in an echo of the Buddhist beliefs, we make the process even more difficult by our addiction to material possessions and our almost pathological identification with our earthly persona, rather than with the Christ consciousness within (i.e. the higher self).

Obtaining this heightened level of awareness and sustaining it while at the same time being grounded in the physical world is something which Jesus wanted everyone on earth to understand as being their divine right. It is believed that Jesus was entrusted with the techniques for attaining altered states of awareness known as merkabah ('rising in the chariot') when he was initiated into the Essenes, an ascetic Jewish mystical sect. But such secrets were not to be freely distributed among the profane, so Jesus and his disciples encoded them in the parables.

A good example of this hidden teaching can be found in the aptly named Book of Revelation, which is traditionally read as an apocalyptic warning of the final battle between good and evil. But knowledge of merkabah (which later evolved into modern Kabbalah) reveals an alternative interpretation.

In describing heaven, or the Holy Jerusalem, the Apostle John talks of there being twelve gates and twelve angels, one for each of the Twelve Tribes of Israel. Kabbalists understand this to be a reference to the twelve human archetypes, each of whom is an expression of one of the divine attributes of the creator. The description of heaven can then be read as a guided visualisation in which the initiate is invited to connect with these twelve divine aspects of himself leading to the awakening of the Christ consciousness within.

In the Gospel of Philip, Jesus is evidently familiar with the astral world, which he refers to as 'the real realm' and 'the realm of truth', and the unity of all things which can be experienced in that state.

> People cannot see anything in the real realm unless they
> become it. In the realm of truth it is not as [with]
> human beings in the world, who see the sun without

> *being the sun... Rather, if you have seen any things*
> *there, you have become those things.*

These apocryphal gospels reveal Jesus as a fully realised human being rather than the one and only Son of God. When he urged his followers to come through him to attain union with the divine he was not, as the Church asserts, demanding obedience, servitude and blind faith, but was instead encouraging us to follow his example.

The promise of a physical resurrection is an invention of the Church. Jesus and his followers made no mention of such a miracle. Instead they spoke of ascending to heaven in spirit, having discarded the physical body upon death or at will during meditation. According to the Gnostic gospels, Jesus appeared to his followers as a spirit to prove that the soul survives death, but due to either selective editing of the Gospels or sloppy translation this central teaching became literalised.

In 1 Corinthians (15:50) and 1 Peter (1:18) it is stated that flesh and blood cannot enter the celestial kingdom while in John 3:13 it is noted that heaven is for spiritual beings and that we are all spirit in essence and will return from whence we came:

> *And no man hath ascended up to heaven, but he that*
> *came down from heaven, even the Son of Man which is*
> *in heaven.*

St Paul attempted to clarify the idea that Jesus had risen physically from the tomb and in so doing made a distinction between our earthly form and our spirit:

> *There are also celestial bodies, and bodies terrestrial:*
> *but the glory of the celestial is one, and the glory of the*
> *terrestrial is another... There is a natural body and*
> *there is a spiritual body.* (1 Corinthians 15:35–44).

In 2 Corinthians, St Paul boasts that he is more spiritual than the other disciples by speaking of his ascent 'in the spirit' to the third heaven, by which traditional Christians understand him to be referring to the empyriam, the presence of God (the first heaven being the physical firmament, the protecting canopy of sky and stars; the second sphere being where the souls of the righteous dwell). But St Paul was an initiate of merkabah and did not intend that his reference to three heavens should be taken literally. In merkabah the three heavens are the three upper worlds of emanation, creation and formation.

Similarly, for many orthodox Christians hell is not symbolic of a state of mind, but a reality, a place of fire and brimstone where the damned are punished for their wickedness on earth or for their rejection of Jesus as their saviour. In crude terms, heaven is for the righteous and hell is for everyone else. But this image of eternal torment and divine retribution is at odds with Jesus' assertion that 'God is Love' and that forgiveness is the greatest gift. The ever-present threat of damnation makes no allowances for human frailty and limits each of us to only one chance at life, which is as impractical as it is irrational – the antithesis of Christian compassion. Jesus acknowledged that everyone makes mistakes when he declared, 'Let he who is without sin cast the first stone'; if heaven were closed to sinners, it would be empty but for the disciples, the martyrs and the saints. Moreover, the belief in hell and the emphasis placed on sin only generates guilt, which is self-defeating – but perhaps that was the intention of those early Christian scholars who selectively edited the Gospels, for without guilt orthodox Christians would have no need of absolution and the clergy who provide it.

> *Jesus said:*
> *'If those who guide your being say to you: "Behold the*
> *Kingdom is in Heaven", then the birds of the sky will*
> *precede you,*
> *if they say to you, "it is in the sea,"*
> *then the fish will precede you.*
> *But the Kingdom is in your centre*
> *And is about you.*
> *When you know your Selves*
> *then you will be known*
> *and you will be aware that you are*
> *the sons of the Living Father.*
> *But if you do not know yourselves*
> *then you are in poverty, and you are the poverty.'*
>
> (Gospel of Thomas)

If modern accounts of near-death experiences are indicative of a natural process or state of being which we all share, then we would expect to find such experiences described in the sacred texts of all the world religions and philosophies, albeit in symbolic form and couched in the cultural context of that period and location. Having made a study of comparative religions, it is my understanding that there is a common concept regarding life after death at the core of all the major religions, but that it has become obscured and confused with the passage of time and by the often wilful misinterpretations and selective editing of scriptures by those who sought to set themselves up as mediators between man and his God. The matter is made worse by the inevitable schisms which resulted in a proliferation of diverse sects each with their own interpretation of the original teachings. In the case of the early Christian Church its founders were accused by the heretical Gnostics of deliberately suppressing certain apocryphal gospels containing Jesus' teachings on reincarnation and karma expressed in such sayings as 'as you sow, so shall you reap' in order to secure the lucrative concession at the gates of heaven.

## Soul travel and the saints

Although the Church had declared reincarnation to be a heresy in 533 AD, it could not expunge belief in spirit travel, especially in those tales told by its own saints. St Augustine (354–430 AD) was disposed to tell the allegedly true story of Senator Curma, whose spirit left his body as he lay in a coma. On hearing his name being called he went in search of other spirits, thinking he had been summoned for the Last Judgement. They told him that it was another man with the same name who was being called to heaven, a goldsmith who lived in the same town. After wandering aimlessly in this netherworld he met other spirits of people who he knew were still alive and were presumably dreaming at that moment. When he finally returned to his body he sent a servant to the house of Curma the goldsmith and was told that the man had died that very day.

Several saints are reputed to have practised the art of astral projection, among them St Severus of Ravenna, St Ambrose and St Clement of Rome. St Anthony of Padua, for example, was said to have been preaching in Limoges, France in 1226 when he remembered that he had agreed to attend a monastery in another part of the town. In full view of the congregation he knelt in silent prayer for several minutes. At the same time he appeared before the monks at the monastery, who heard him read the lesson as he had promised. He then vanished before their eyes. Centuries later, in 1774, St Alphonsus Liguori collapsed during Mass and remained unconscious for 24 hours. On recovering he claimed to have been present at the death of Pope Clement XIV in Rome. His story was later verified by those who saw him praying at the bedside of the dying pontiff. Such stories may strike the non-believer as prime examples of Catholic mythology, but the phenomenon of bilocation, to use its scientific term, is not uncommon (see Into the Light – Living Apparitions, page 55).

# 3

# Altered States

*There are mysteries that are meant to be solved and there are mysteries that are meant to be explored.*

(Kenneth Ring)

## The dream dimension

There are some dreams which seem so real that we have difficulty adjusting to the 'real world' when we wake. For a few moments we appear disorientated and out of focus in our bodies, a state that cannot be explained as simple tiredness. Often we say to ourselves or members of our family, 'I could have sworn that was real.' The memory of such dreams often lasts for days in contrast to those which drain away the instant we open our eyes. So what is the significance of these dreams and is it possible that in our deepest sleep we experience the first stage of death?

In such dreams we find ourselves totally immersed in a believable world, our surroundings appear solid and we have a sense of space, of moving through the environment as if we were walking or travelling by conventional means. But – and I believe that this is the most significant clue to the temporary nature of this particular reality – we never have any memory of being our waking self. We never recall our home or the particulars of our waking life. We only do this in the shallow end of sleep, in which we act out our anxieties and aspirations. But during our deepest dreams we are 'away' on a visit to a strangely familiar environment that has no basis in our waking life. In these dreams we are our true selves and as such do not identify with the life that we have literally left behind us when we leave our body. There is thus an important distinction to be made between ordinary mundane dreams in which we re-run events of the previous day and which are characterised by a distinctive surreal quality and these spirit dreams of an alternative reality.

Several students attending my meditation courses have told me of dream meetings with loved ones who died many years before and they were convinced that these reunions were real. It is my opinion that they *are* real and that they are possible because in the deepest stages of sleep we can travel in our dream body to a realm between the worlds and it is in this state that we can create our idyll, which many mediums have interpreted as heaven.

It is my understanding that this heaven of landscaped gardens and beautiful marble buildings is not a real location but a state of mind, of awareness, in which we create our own environment through the faculty of the imagination. But it is only a transitional state between the physical world and the higher realm to which we gravitate once we have cast off our emotional attachments and desires. It is the bardo of which the Buddhists speak – not the pastoral paradise beyond the tunnel of light, which is accompanied by a sensation of bliss and from which all who have experienced it are reluctant to return. In this netherworld we linger for as long as it takes to lose our attachment to earthly things. It is for this reason that the recently deceased rarely reveal any significant insights into the nature of existence or the purpose of life when communicating through a medium but are instead preoccupied with mundane matters or talk in vague terms of the importance of loving one another. This is because they are just on the other side of life in the bardo, this false heaven, not in the higher realms.

It always struck me as curious that no one older than a grandparent will communicate through a medium. Presumably older souls have long since moved on to higher states or been reincarnated.

## Lucid dreaming

The possibility that we may leave our bodies temporarily during the deepest stages of sleep was first suggested by the Dutch physicist Frederick Van Eeden in 1904. Van Eeden coined the term 'lucid dreaming' to describe the phenomenon in which the dreamer becomes aware that they are dreaming and then takes control of the dream, experiencing all the sensations of a normal OBE but within the fanciful landscape created by the unconscious mind. It appears to be a very common experience and is triggered by the realisation that the situation in the dream is too unlikely for it to be real, such as when adults find themselves back at school sitting exams. At some point the conscious mind kicks in, reminding the dreamer that this scenario is impossible, but instead of opening their eyes they wake up in their 'dream body' and can then manipulate the landscape of the dream world at will.

Lucid dreams invariably involve the sensation of flying, because the 'dream body' is floating free of the physical, and they usually come to an end with a sensation of falling as the dreamer returns to their physical body with a jolt.

In one particularly memorable dream van Eeden dreamt that he was looking out of a window and wondered how he could be in two places at once because he knew for a fact that he was really at home in bed. So he decided to try to wake up slowly and note the transition from awareness of the dream world to that of the 'real' world, whilst observing how the sensation of lying on his stomach in the dream would change into the sensation of lying on his back in reality. As he did so he sensed a 'wonderful' shift as his awareness slipped from one body into the other. 'There is a distinct recollection of the two bodies,' he observed, 'It is so much beyond doubt that it leads almost unavoidably to the concept of a dream body.'

Habitual lucid dreamers, who claim to be able to induce the state at will, speak of hearing 'wise inner voices' that offer guidance to help resolve problems in their waking lives. They also claim that their ability to manipulate their environment increases with experience.

If you wish to induce a lucid dream, the exercise on page 130 in Chapter 9 offers a safe technique with which you can experiment.

## Glimpsing a greater reality

If we wish to free ourselves from the fear of death we need to accept the simple fact that nothing dies and that it is only the illusion of separation that creates suffering.

'Everything is alive, there is nothing dead, it is only we who are dead,' observed Pyotr Ouspensky (1878–1947), the Russian mystic whose revelational visions suggest that heaven and its inhabitants are all around us, but that we are too preoccupied with mundane matters to realise that they are there.

Ouspensky's insights were induced by the occasional ingestion of nitrous oxide, which he claimed produced a heightened awareness that was in contrast to the hallucinogenic dreams created by narcotics. The use of the non-toxic gas was considered a legitimate adjunct to meditation in the early years of the last century by certain members of the intellectual elite, including America's foremost philosopher, William James, who declared:

> Depth beyond depth of truth seem revealed to the inhaler... the sense of a profound meaning having been there persists; and I know more than one person who is persuaded that in the nitrous oxide trance we have a genuine metaphysical revelation.

James' unqualified endorsement and Ouspensky's mystical experiences encouraged many to experiment in the hope of sharing their awakening to the duality of the self and the realisation that every particle in existence is alive and interconnected, that even inanimate objects are suffused with residual personal energy.

Ouspensky's awakening involved the realisation that he was both the physical person he saw in the mirror and at the same time something much greater. This superior aspect he called the 'higher self'. And it was in this heightened state of awareness that he perceived meaning in all things, even familiar household objects. Looking through the eyes of the higher self he could see the processes that had brought the object into being and the chain of events that had brought it into his presence. Everyone who had touched the object had left an echo of their personal energy upon it. Nothing was isolated or truly inanimate.

But in opening himself to direct communication with the higher self he was overwhelmed by the flood of impressions which made it impossible to complete even a single sentence describing what he had seen. Even if he had been able to quieten his mind he admitted it would have been impossible to express everything in words. Language is simply inadequate to convey what is beyond human comprehension. Our perception of 'reality' is limited to whatever stimuli we process through our five physical senses – touch, taste, sound, sight and smell. We need to develop a sixth sense if we are to perceive more subtle impressions.

It was Ouspensky's conclusion that a man could go mad by looking at a single ashtray. Everything was an indispensable particle in the pattern of existence and this notion rendered him incapable of feeling indifferent. Particularly interesting were old buildings, which retained the thoughts, feelings, moods and memories of their present and previous inhabitants. He likened the inhabitants to the various aspects of our own personalities, which make way each time we bring another quality or persona to the fore. When observing a cat or dog he became aware that they were personifications of an idea and that the nature of the animal found expression in its form. A dog was more than flesh, blood and bones; it was a combination of atoms and consciousness that assumed a form that best expressed its nature. Similarly, human beings were atoms in the body of a greater being.

This sense of the 'rightness of things', of everything conforming to a cosmic pattern and unfolding to a will greater than the individual, diminished as he re-experienced the oppressive ordinariness of the physical world.

> The strangest thing in all these experiences was the coming back, the return to the ordinary state we call life. This was something very similar to dying or to what we thought dying must be.

# Man and superman

A similar state was attained by J.G.Bennett, biographer and student of the Russian mystic G.I. Gurdjieff (1873–1949), who had also taught Ouspensky. Bennett had been practising a series of demanding physical and psycho-spiritual exercises designed to confound the automaton of our ordinary mind or ego, allowing the higher self to take over. But it had left him exhausted and ill. The next morning he had a high temperature and was reluctant to get out of bed. At that moment of surrender he found himself 'possessed' by a superior will that took over his body and led him to rise and dress himself. He was in a state of acute alertness as if he had tuned in to a higher frequency. He felt exhilarated and immortal, like a divine being that had taken command of a new body, one charged with an inexhaustible power source and somehow beyond the purely physical mechanics of movement. There was no conscious effort or sense of exertion as he joined the morning exercise class. Before long the others had dropped out with exhaustion leaving Bennett to test the limits of the superior self that had taken him over. His description sounds remarkably similar to that given by those who have observed their etheric body during an OBE:

> I was filled with the influx of an immense power. My
> body seemed to have turned into light... There was no
> effort, no pain, no weariness, not even any sense of
> weight.

After the class he went into the grounds of Gurdjieff's spiritual training college and dug in the garden for an hour, in an unmerciful heat and at a pace that would have exhausted a younger man in considerably better physical condition.

In the midst of his exertions he experienced a heightened sense of awareness in which he perceived the unity of everything he looked at. Every object, every person he saw had its place and purpose in existence, although he struggled to express the ineffable sense of the fifth dimension in which he now existed. At one point he exclaimed, 'Now I see why God hides Himself from us.' But at that moment he could not have explained the intuition behind this insight had anyone asked him for one.

He remained on such a 'high' that he could not rest, so instead he went for a walk in the forest and marvelled at the 'eternal pattern' that he saw in the intricate tapestry that nature had arranged before him. In a state of exhilaration he recalled a description of the mystical state by Ouspensky, in which he stated that we have no control over our emotions. At that moment Bennett willed himself to be astonished and was overwhelmed with the uniqueness of each and every tree. He then thought of 'fear' and began to shake with terror at imagined horrors in the shadows. With the thought of 'joy' the fear instantly evaporated and he was overcome with a feeling of elation.

Finally, he thought of 'love' and was so overwhelmed with such fine shades of tenderness and compassion that he realised that he had not the remotest idea of the depth and range of love in the universal sense. Love was everywhere and in everything. This acute sensitivity soon became too intense and Bennett feared that if he explored this emotion any further he would cease to exist. In that moment he realised why an awareness of the greater reality is filtered out by the five physical senses. He chose to lose this new-found ability to awaken specific emotions at will, and in the next instant it left him.

## Huxley and the doors of perception

A similar insight opened the doors of perception for author Aldous Huxley. On a bright May morning in 1953 Huxley ingested a minute dosage of mescaline in water and sat back in expectation. He believed that if the new generation of mind-expanding drugs were taken by intellectuals in the pursuit of enlightenment they would be privileged to 'a sense of solidarity with the world and its spiritual principle'.

Mescaline promised to reveal 'the ultimate reality' without the attendant side effects of LSD, as it was derived from peyote, a natural hallucinogenic that the Native American shamans had been using for centuries.

> *I had expected to lie with my eyes shut, looking at visions of many coloured geometries, of animated architectures, rich with gems and fabulously lovely, of landscapes with heroic figures, of symbolic dramas trembling perpetually on the verge of the ultimate revelation. But I had not reckoned, it was evident, with the idiosyncrasies of my mental make-up, the facts of my temperament, training and habits.*

To Huxley's consternation, it was not the inner world that was illuminated, but the outer. Instead of the mystical visions of which he had read, the walls of his self-centred world crumbled before him revealing an intensity of existence he could never have imagined. Everything, from a vase of flowers to the creases in his trousers, became wonders of infinite complexity.

> *A bunch of flowers shining with their own inner light...*
> *Those folds – what a labyrinth of endless significant complexity! ... I was seeing what Adam had seen on the*

*morning of his own creation – the miracle, moment by
moment, of naked existence.*

Huxley's experience led him to conclude that our senses are
deliberately dulled, or rather that our perception of 'reality' is the result of
information being filtered by our brains, in order that we can function as
higher animals in the physical world. Otherwise, our senses would be
overwhelmed. As he observed:

*The mind was primarily concerned, not with measures
and locations, but with being and meaning ... In the
intervals between his revelations the mescaline taker is
apt to feel that, though in one way everything is
supremely as it should be, in another there is something
wrong.*

What Huxley considered 'wrong' was the sense of separateness that
mescaline induced. Only through raising our consciousness naturally, and
not artificially with drugs, can we attain the sense of unity experienced by
mystics and philosophers. If we can do that, he argued, then we will have
truly opened the doors of perception.

# 4

# Through the Veil – the Moment of Death

What is it like to die? The answer to that perennial question can be readily answered by the many thousands of people around the world who claim to have had a near-death experience. For those who recall slipping out of their physical shell as effortlessly as a snake sheds its skin, of floating free and experiencing the sensation of flying vast distances at the speed of thought, it is more real than our world of form and matter.

Prior to the nineteenth century such experiences were thought to be the province of religious visionaries, but the growing interest in spiritualism during the Victorian era and the possibility that science might be able to explain certain paranormal phenomena created an intense interest in psychical research.

One of the first to make a serious study of such phenomena was Professor Albert Helm, a Swiss geologist and avid mountain climber whose interest stemmed from his own brush with death.

During a precarious climb in the Alps in 1871 the professor lost his footing and plunged to what he thought was his death.

> *What followed was a series of singularly clear flashes of thought between a rapid, profuse succession of images that were sharp and distinct... I can perhaps compare it best to images from film sprung loose in a projector or with a rapid sequence of dream images. As though I looked out of the window of a high house, I saw myself as a seven-year-old boy going to school. Then I saw myself in the classroom with my beloved teacher Weisz in the fourth grade. I acted out my life, as though I was an actor on a stage, upon which I looked down as though from practically the highest gallery in the*

*theatre. I was both hero and onlooker... I had the*
*feeling of submission to necessity. Then I saw arching*
*over me – my eyes were directed upwards – a beautiful*
*blue heaven with small violet and rosy-red clouds. Then*
*sounded solemn music, as though from an organ, in*
*powerful chords... I felt myself go softly backwards into*
*this magnificent heaven – without anxiety, without*
*grief. It was a great, glorious moment!*

The experience prompted Helm to question other climbers who had narrowly escaped death and in 1892 he published the first article on the subject of what is now commonly called the near-death experience. From this study he was able to identify several significant elements which occurred in each and every account he had been given: the sense of existing in a moment beyond time, the life review unfolding as if one were a spectator observing one's own life, and the blissful all-enveloping peace in place of the terror one would have expected.

Professor Helm experienced a spontaneous separation of mind and body with the shock realisation that his death was imminent, but usually the individual will become aware that they are looking down on their body after suffering a near-fatal accident, a critical illness, or after being put under the influence of anaesthetic.

One man who remained fully conscious during the process of death itself, and was revived in time to describe his thoughts and sensations in detail, was not the sort of person one might expect to admit having had such an experience.

The Reverend Bertrand told his story to two of the most respected paranormal researchers of the Victorian period, Richard Hodgson and William James, who conscientiously verified the facts with the witnesses before publishing the case in the *Journal of Psychical Research* in 1892.

Reverend Bertrand had been climbing a mountain in the Alps with a party of students when he began to feel weak. He had seen the summit on several previous occasions so he had no regrets as he waved them on their way and sat down to smoke a cigar. But as he struck a match he realised that he couldn't move his hands. In fact, he couldn't move at all. He was freezing to death. His first instinct was to pray, but afterwards he simply surrendered to the inevitable and decided to observe the process of his own death with clinical detachment.

When the numbing cold gripped his head he felt himself separating from his body. From his new perspective he was able to look down on the petrified figure with the match still held between his frozen fingers. Then he noticed that he was connected to his body by what he described as an elastic string, which allowed him to rise into the air like a balloon. Up he went, exultant at being free from cold and pain. From here he caught sight of the other climbers and noted that the guide was taking the right-hand path to the summit against his explicit instructions. He also observed the guide eating a chicken leg and taking a drink from the provisions he had lent him. 'Go on, old fellow', he heard himself say, 'eat the whole chicken if you choose, for I hope my miserable corpse will never eat or drink again.'

Leaving the mountain behind he drifted further until he hovered over the nearby town of Lungren, where he saw his wife alighting from a carriage with four other travellers and entering a hotel in search of refreshments. At this point the only feeling he had other than the sensation of liberation was a faint regret that he could not sever the cord and be free for ever. But in the next instant he was jerked back towards his body where the guide was vigorously massaging him in an attempt to restore the circulation. Death was effortless and painless compared to his return to life.

> *I had a hope – the balloon seemed much too big for the mouth. Suddenly I uttered an awful roar like a wild beast; the corpse swallowed the balloon, and Bertrand was Bertrand again.*

If the guide had expected to be rewarded for his efforts he must have been sorely disappointed. Bertrand berated him for taking the more dangerous route and for helping himself to his food and drink. On his return to Lucerne, Bertrand was met by his wife who was taken aback to be asked why she had made an unscheduled stop at Lungren with her four travelling companions.

# Out of the body

A number of individuals have attempted to describe the sensation of being in their etheric body. Some liken it to a cloud of colours and others to an energy field, while one man took the opportunity to look closely at his hands and described them as being composed of light connected by a network of vein-like structures and tubes, which sounds similar to the meridian lines connecting the chakras, or subtle energy centres of Hindu philosophy. Even the whorls of his fingerprints were visible, highlighted by the radiance within.

## Larsen – the girl in the mirror

A more detailed description of what the astral body looks like was given by Caroline Larsen, a middle-aged Vermont housewife who was sufficiently curious to look in a mirror during her OBE which took place one autumn evening in 1910.

The episode had been preceded by inexplicable anxiety, as if she could sense that something strange was about to occur, so she had lain down on her bed and tried to relax. But despite her best efforts she succumbed to what she later described as an overpowering oppression and then a paralysis which left her numb from head to toe. In the next instant she was standing at the foot of her bed looking back at her own body with idle curiosity. She noted that everything in the room appeared just as it had been when she had lain down on the bed. The colours of the carpet, wallpaper and ornaments were all as they should have been. But on entering the bathroom she instinctively reached for the light switch and was surprised that she couldn't make physical contact with it. But she stopped trying as soon as she realised that the room was illuminated by her own inner radiance, sufficiently so for her to look in a full-length mirror. What she saw there remained with her for the rest of her life.

In place of a middle-aged woman was a girl of about 18 years of age similar to the way Mrs Larsen had looked in her youth, but more beautiful and with skin like alabaster. Her face and limbs were transparent with a darker substance running through the centre of the arms, hands and fingers comparable to the bones seen in x-ray plates.

Her eyes were 'piercingly keen' and her hair, which had recently turned grey, cascaded in soft, brown waves as it had in her younger years. To her delight she noted that she was dressed in a sleeveless one-piece garment which radiated with a soft suffused glow.

The image she describes may sound like an ageing person's fantasy, but there are innumerable accounts of spectral sightings in which the deceased returns in an idealised form, free from the illness or disability from which they suffered in life. The *Tibetan Book of the Dead* states that the form in which the deceased often appears is a projection of their self-image. They are so used to having a physical body that they cannot imagine themselves without one.

## Gerhardie – not his accustomed self

'I neither drink nor take drugs,' declared British author and playwright William Gerhardie in his semi-autobiographical novel *Resurrection*, published in 1934. 'All I brought to my bed was a considerable nervous exhaustion which sleep was required to restore.' Gerhardie's assertion was made in anticipation of the derision that he expected would greet his claim to have had what is now commonly referred to as an OBE. But he need not have worried. In the years following the Great War interest in psychic phenomena was at its height, as bereaved families throughout Europe grasped at the vaguest promise of being able to see their fallen sons, brothers, fathers, uncles, nephews, neighbours and friends again. People wanted to believe in the possibility of life after death.

Nevertheless, Gerhardie feared that his claim would taint his reputation as a serious writer and so during the experience itself he made a conscious effort to note every significant detail, which he could verify after he had returned to his body. It is for this reason that his account remains one of the most persuasive and compelling descriptions of the astral state on record.

Although he had no knowledge of such phenomena prior to his own experience, Gerhardie was surprisingly calm and more than a little curious when he found himself suspended in the air that night looking down on his own body lying in bed. 'Now this *is* something to tell,' he said to himself. 'And this is *not* a dream.' Being of an inquisitive nature he seized on it as an opportunity to explore the condition and his environment. After remaining suspended for a few minutes he floated down to land on his feet, at which point he became aware that he was connected to his physical body by a cord of light, which he compared to the penetrating beam from a movie projector. The far end of the beam was attached to his forehead and was sufficiently bright to illuminate his sleeping self, breathing peacefully. Seeing himself in this way was fascinating as it was quite a different perspective from looking in a mirror. The placid features and steady breathing reassured Gerhardie that he was not dead, but neither was he his 'accustomed self'. This new body, though light as a bubble, took some getting used to. He didn't have to move his limbs to manoeuvre around his apartment, he only had to will himself to see another room and he would pass through the door like a ghost, which is in effect what he was at that moment: a living apparition.

> ... it was as if my mould was walking through a murky
> heavy space which, however, gave way easily before my
> emptiness.

All the while he experienced an exhilaration coupled with a faint anxiety that the cord might be severed. It was this fear that drew him back to hover over his body, but the prospect of losing his new-found freedom was so great that he overcame his unease and willed himself to continue his astral excursion. He observed that whenever he travelled at speed his consciousness would 'blot out' and only return when he moved at a reasonable speed.

Another peculiar feature of this spectral body double was the fact that it emitted a soft warm glow that was sufficiently bright for him to explore the otherwise dark apartment and note details for subsequent verification. Gerhardie was determined to prove to himself that this extraordinary experience was not a dream. With that in mind he drifted from room to room observing which windows were open and if the curtains were drawn; he also noted the position of certain ornaments. Eager to venture further he passed through the front door which was closed and found himself outside. It was at this point that his apprehension returned and he looked back to reassure himself that the silver cord was still there. It was, but it had stretched so thin that Gerhardie became anxious and this snapped him back into his body with a jolt. As he later commented, every detail was still vivid in his mind.

> ...and there was quite another quality about it all, that of reality, which removed it from the mere memory of a dream.

He rose and went through the apartment confirming what he had observed while travelling in his astral body,

> and the evidence in all cases proved correct.

The experience left Gerhardie's previously held beliefs on the subject of life after death in tatters.

## Geddes – the psychic stream

One of the most reliable descriptions of the astral experience was offered to members of the Royal Medical Society by Professor of Anatomy Sir Auckland Geddes in 1937. Geddes attributed the experience to an anonymous colleague, but it is thought that he was relating a personal experience and that he feared for his reputation if he admitted as much.

According to Geddes, while the man was confined to bed with a fever he had the distinct impression that his mind was separating into its component parts; one being the intellect and the other being physical awareness, which was firmly grounded in the body. He experienced a shift in his perspective until he was observing his ailing body with detached interest from the other side of the room. In this non-corporeal state he became aware that the only reality was the current moment, in which 'here' and 'now' were the only true states of being.

The human brain, he realised, was the physical receptacle of a 'psychic stream' which saturates this fifth dimension. While we are grounded in the material world we are attuned to the lowest vibrational frequency, but when our consciousness is raised through contemplation, or in the ecstasy of a peak experience, we can become conscious of these other realities as if we had retuned to a higher wavelength.

His new found psychic sight enabled Geddes' colleague to observe the multicoloured auras of energy surrounding the living whom he could still see and hear although they were unaware of his presence, an experience he compared to being underwater in a giant aquarium.

His exploration of the fifth dimension was abruptly terminated when a friend entered his room and, finding him in a comatose state, immediately called a doctor. In the same instant the anonymous 'physician' saw the doctor receiving the emergency call and witnessed the efforts made to resuscitate him.

As he was drawn back into his body he became 'intensely annoyed' at the prospect of being confined once again in the cold clay of his physical shell. 'I was so interested and was just beginning to understand where I was and what I was seeing,' he remarked.

## Acharya – our spirit twin

> It is a pity so few remember what they do at night; if they did, they would be much less troubled about the state they call death... and the wicked rumours circulated concerning hell and eternal damnation would have no more effect on them than [does] the fear of the ogre in the children's fairy book [affect] the adult reader.

These words were spoken in July 1941 by Acharya, an Indian guru, in answer to the despair voiced by Peter Richelieu, a South African, who was grieving for the loss of his brother who had recently been killed in action. In his autobiographical *A Soul's Journey*, Richelieu states that Acharya appeared as if in answer to a prayer to reveal the mysteries of life and death, which included learning how to leave his body and explore the astral world. As Acharya explained:

> The ego wears each of these bodies like a layer of clothes, and, in death, each one falls away as we leave the denser worlds of matter behind – assuming that we can detach ourselves from the physical world. If our emotional attachments or desires are too strong, or if we cannot accept death, we may linger on the astral plane, appearing to the living as ghosts. The mental and astral bodies are of finite matter which, when drawn about us, take on the impression of the physical body which is the reason ghosts are recognisable when seen by the living.

Acharya went on to describe another layer of the physical body – its spirit 'twin' – the 'etheric' double, which surrounds our nerve system and acts as a conductor of the nerve currents. Although he didn't allude to it, this is the 'sympathetic' network of nerves in the etheric double on which spiritual healers and acupuncturists effect their cures. He added:

> The young soul, or un-evolved ego, certainly gets out of his body during sleep – he cannot help doing so – but his intelligence (mental mind or body) is not sufficiently

*developed... therefore he usually hangs about near his*
*sleep body waiting for the call to re-enter it.*

On a subsequent visit, Acharya described what happens at the moment of death. The etheric double knows that death of the physical body means death for itself too, and so clings to the astral body, sustaining itself on the life force. Through an effort of will, the dying person must detach himself from this last connection with the physical world, or else he will find himself suspended between the two worlds.

*Men who die fearing death often refuse to make the*
*necessary effort of will ... in the hope of continuing their*
*physical existence, the physical life being the only one*
*they know.*

Richelieu's anxieties were dispelled as Acharya explained how our thoughts and actions in life determine our experiences after death.

*There is no reward, no punishment, but there is result,*
*there is cause and effect and the law acts just as much*
*in higher worlds as it acts down here on the physical*
*plane. As we live now and as we are now, so shall we be*
*on the other side of death. And our life there will be*
*conditioned by the thoughts with which we have*
*surrounded ourselves down here. As the astral world is*
*a world of illusion ... everything ... is produced by*
*thought.*

## Jung – a vision of liberation or a new reality

Anyone who regards such experiences as irrational might care to consider the fact that modern analytical psychology evolved from the personal experiences of its founder, Carl Jung, who experienced a profound out-of-body state after suffering a heart attack in 1944. The insights his experience reveals of our true nature and the subjective nature of reality make this excerpt from his autobiographical *Memories, Dreams, Reflections* worth reproducing at length. Incidentally, Jung considered the Hindu figure he describes in the narrative to be an archetypal personification of his higher self.

*It seemed to me that I was high up in space. Far below*
*I saw the globe of the earth, bathed in a gloriously blue*
*light. I saw the deep blue sea and the continents. Far*
*below my feet lay Ceylon, and in the distance ahead of*
*me the subcontinent of India. My field of vision did not*
*include the whole earth, but its global shape was*

*plainly distinguishable and its outlines shone with a silvery gleam through that wonderful blue light. In many places the globe seemed colored, or spotted dark green like oxidized silver. Far away to the left lay a broad expanse – the reddish-yellow desert of Arabia; it was as though the silver of the earth had there assumed a reddish-gold hue. Then came the Red Sea, and far, far back – as if in the upper left of a map – I could just make out a bit of the Mediterranean. My gaze was directed chiefly toward that. Everything else appeared indistinct. I could also see the snow-covered Himalayas, but in that direction it was foggy or cloudy. I did not look to the right at all. I knew that I was on the point of departing from the earth.*

*Later I discovered how high in space one would have to be to have so extensive a view – approximately a thousand miles! The sight of the earth from this height was the most glorious thing I had ever seen.*

*After contemplating it for a while, I turned around. I had been standing with my back to the Indian Ocean, as it were, and my face to the north. Then it seemed to me that I made a turn to the south. Something new entered my field of vision. A short distance away I saw in space a tremendous dark block of stone, like a meteorite. It was about the size of my house, or even bigger. It was floating in space, and I myself was floating in space.*

*I had seen similar stones on the coast of the Gulf of Bengal. They were blocks of tawny granite, and some of them had been hollowed out into temples. My stone was one such gigantic dark block. An entrance led into a small antechamber. To the right of the entrance, a black Hindu sat silently in lotus posture upon a stone bench. He wore a white gown, and I knew that he expected me. Two steps led up to this antechamber, and inside, on the left, was the gate to the temple. Innumerable tiny niches, each with a saucer-like concavity filled with coconut oil and small burning wicks, surrounded the door with a wreath of bright flames. I had once actually seen this when I visited the Temple of the Holy Tooth at Kandy in Ceylon; the gate had been framed by several rows of burning oil lamps of this sort.*

*As I approached the steps leading up to the entrance into the rock, a strange thing happened: I had the feeling that everything was being sloughed away; everything I aimed at or wished for or thought, the whole phantasmagoria of earthly existence, fell away or was stripped from me – an extremely painful process. Nevertheless something remained; it was as if I now carried along with me everything I had ever experienced or done, everything that had happened around me. I might also say: it was with me, and I was it. I consisted of all that, so to speak. I consisted of my own history and I felt with great certainty: this is what I am. I am this bundle of what has been and what has been accomplished.*

*This experience gave me a feeling of extreme poverty, but at the same time of great fullness. There was no longer anything I wanted or desired. I existed in an objective form; I was what I had been and lived. At first the sense of annihilation predominated, of having been stripped or pillaged; but suddenly that became of no consequence.*

*Everything seemed to be past; what remained was a 'fait accompli', without any reference back to what had been. There was no longer any regret that something had dropped away or been taken away. On the contrary: I had everything that I was, and that was everything.*

*Something else engaged my attention: as I approached the temple I had the certainty that I was about to enter an illuminated room and would meet there all those people to whom I belong in reality. There I would at last understand – this too was a certainty – what historical nexus I or my life fitted into. I would know what had been before me, why I had come into being, and where my life was flowing. My life as I lived it had often seemed to me like a story that has no beginning and end. I had the feeling that I was a historical fragment, an excerpt for which the preceding and succeeding text*

51

*was missing. My life seemed to have been snipped out of a long chain of events, and many questions had remained unanswered. Why had it taken this course? Why had I brought these particular assumptions with me? What had I made of them? What will follow? I felt sure that I would receive an answer to all the questions as soon as I entered the rock temple. There I would meet the people who knew the answer to my question about what had been before and what would come after.*

*While I was thinking over these matters, something happened that caught my attention. From below, from the direction of Europe, an image floated up. It was my doctor, or rather, his likeness – framed by a golden chain or a golden laurel wreath. I knew at once: 'Aha, this is my doctor, of course, the one who has been treating me. But now he is coming in his primal form. In life he was an avatar of the temporal embodiment of the primal form, which has existed from the beginning. Now he is appearing in that primal form.'*

*Presumably I too was in my primal form, though this was something I did not observe but simply took for granted. As he stood before me, a mute exchange of thought took place between us. The doctor had been delegated by the earth to deliver a message to me, to tell me that there was a protest against my going away. I had no right to leave the earth and must return. The moment I heard that, the vision ceased.*

*I was profoundly disappointed, for now it all seemed to have been for nothing. The painful process of defoliation had been in vain, and I was not to be allowed to enter the temple, to join the people in whose company I belonged.*

*In reality, a good three weeks were still to pass before I could truly make up my mind to live again. I could not eat because all food repelled me. The view of city and mountains from my sickbed seemed to me like a painted curtain with black holes in it, or a tattered sheet of newspaper full of photographs that meant nothing. Disappointed, I thought, 'Now I must return to the "box system" again.' For it seemed to me as if behind the horizon of the cosmos a three-dimensional world had been artificially built up, in which each person sat by himself in a little box. And now I should have to convince myself all over again that this was important! Life and the whole world struck me as a prison, and it bothered me beyond measure that I should again be finding all that quite in order. I had been so glad to shed it all, and now it had come about that I – along with everyone else – would again be hung up in a box by a thread.*

*I felt violent resistance to my doctor because he had brought me back to life. At the same time, I was worried about him. 'His life is in danger, for heaven's sake! He has appeared to me in his primal form! When anybody attains this form it means he is going to die, for already he belongs to the "greater company".' Suddenly the terrifying thought came to me that the doctor would have to die in my stead. I tried my best to talk to him about it, but he did not understand me. Then I became angry with him.*

*In actual fact I was his last patient. On April 4, 1944 – I still remember the exact date I was allowed to sit up on the edge of my bed for the first time since the beginning of my illness, and on this same day the doctor took to his bed and did not leave it again. I heard that he was having intermittent attacks of fever. Soon afterward he died of septicemia. He was a good doctor; there was something of the genius about him. Otherwise he would not have appeared to me as an avatar of the temporal embodiment of the primal form.*

# A meeting of ghosts

Although the majority of astral excursions involve an exploration of familiar surroundings from a new perspective, it is perhaps inevitable that sooner or later the frequent traveller will meet with other disembodied souls, some of them permanent residents of this misty netherworld.

Robert Monroe, a leading authority on OBE phenomena and founder of the Mind Research Institute in Virginia, has written of such an incident which hadn't disturbed him at the time but which later gave him cause for reflection. He had just fallen asleep in a house that he had been renting when he felt himself float free of his body. It was a familiar pleasant sensation and he was anticipating having the freedom to explore when he noticed a white form hovering in the doorway. As he focused upon it he could discern the shape and features of a middle-aged woman of average height with straight dark hair and deep-set eyes. As they exchanged glances he became aware that he could see right through her to the windows and the curtains behind. She gave him a weak smile and left the room.

A few days later Monroe met his new neighbour, a psychiatrist by the name of Dr Kahn, who informed him that the former owner of the house, a Mrs W., was deceased. He offered to produce a photograph if Monroe thought that he might be able to identify his ghostly visitor, and duly did so. There were 50 or 60 people in the photograph and to Dr Kahn's surprise Monroe unhesitatingly picked out Mrs W.

# 5

# Into the Light – Living Apparitions

Although both OBEs and NDEs are invariably the result of a physical, mental or emotional crisis of some kind and almost always when the body is inactive, there are rare cases when the spirit has separated during normal waking life.

The Oxford researcher Celia Green recorded one such case during a study for the Institute of Psychophysical Research in 1968. The subject was a waitress who had been working a 12-hour shift without sleep. She missed the last bus and so determined to walk the fifteen minutes to her home, despite chronic fatigue. As she walked she felt like an automaton moving in a neutral gear with no sense of physical effort or intent. The next thing she registered was hearing the hollow sound of her heels on the pavement and the realisation that she was looking down on herself from across the street. She had no previous knowledge of OBEs but knew intuitively that the part of her that was outside her body was 'the part that counts'. She remembered thinking, 'so that's how I look to other people'.

Another of Green's interviewees described this new-found sense of completeness as 'the real me'. Again, this is a characteristic that distinguishes the OBE from a dream.

Dr Robert Crookall, a noted English researcher into the OBE phenomenon, recorded the case of a mother who sensed that her newly married daughter had fallen sick during a sea voyage and in her concern unconsciously projected her body across the ocean to give the girl some motherly advice. The daughter later wrote to her mother in a state of mild shock describing the moment she had been visited by the living apparition and detailing the conversation between them, all of which corroborated the mother's story down to the precise time of the meeting.

Even more notable is an incident recorded by Sylvan Muldoon, author of *The Phenomena of Astral Projection* (1970), in which a young farmer concerned for his father's health visited the old man's home in his spirit body and on his return noted the time and other significant details. The young farmer, Walter MacBride of Indiana, was struck by the fact that his father appeared to be aware of his presence: the old man looked directly at his unexpected guest with mild surprise on his face. Two days later on Christmas Day, Walter visited his father in person and was intrigued to learn that he too had noted the time and other details, all of which corresponded in every way. Furthermore, the written account of the incident sent to Muldoon was accompanied by a letter verifying the story signed by a Mrs Wires and her son who had been present when Walter visited his father that Christmas Day.

A recurring theme in the numerous recorded incidents of 'phantom forerunners', as they are sometimes called, is the desire on the part of the individual to be at another location and their ability to imagine themselves being there.

The Russian novelist Leo Tolstoy lent credibility to the belief when he wrote of a fateful meeting with celebrated British medium Daniel Douglas Home. Tolstoy and his wife were waiting at the St Petersburg railway station to greet their guest when they saw Home alight from the train and walk away without acknowledging them. Somewhat annoyed they decided to write a note to the hotel where he was staying expressing their irritation at his discourtesy. Home was surprised to receive the note when he finally checked in three hours later. He had not been on the earlier train but had arrived after the Tolstoys had returned home.

Some individuals appear to be more predisposed to the projection of their mind in this manner than others. In an earlier book, *Investigating The Unexplained*, I describe the well-documented case of Emilie Sagée, a young French schoolteacher whose doppelganger (body double) was seen on several occasions by her students and employers in one part of the school while her physical body was in another. One inquisitive pupil even plucked up the courage to touch Mlle Sagée's double and discovered that her hand passed right though the spectral schoolteacher whose body felt like muslin. Not surprisingly, her unconscious ability unnerved her colleagues who pressured the governors to dismiss her and she moved from school to school – one a year for the next 16 years – until she finally took early retirement.

## Deathbed visions

Towards the end of the nineteenth century respectable scientists began to make serious studies of paranormal phenomena and in particular, the greatest mystery of all – proving the existence of life after death. Those who considered themselves too lofty to expose the theatrical antics of the fake mediums found a respectable alternative, recording deathbed visions. These have proven insightful.

One of the first notable studies of the subject was conducted by the eminent physicist Sir William Barrett of the Royal College of Science in Dublin. During a bitter winter's night in January 1924, Lady Barrett, who was an obstetrician, attended a woman who later died after giving birth. The Barretts withheld the mother's surname so we only know her by her forename, Doris. As Doris was dying she gazed into a corner of the room and broke into a radiant smile. 'Lovely, lovely,' she gasped. 'Lovely brightness – wonderful beings'. Then she cried out in joyful surprise, 'Why, it's Father! Oh, he's so glad I'm coming; he is so glad.'

But when she was handed her baby her euphoria faded and she expressed doubt as to whether she should give up her fight for life so readily. But on turning back towards her father (whom Lady Barrett could not see) she reaffirmed her determination to go, saying 'I can't – I can't stay. I am coming.' Then as she died she exclaimed, 'He has Vida with him,' in a tone of surprise and disbelief. It was only later that the Barretts learnt that Vida was Doris's sister and that she had died three weeks earlier, but this news had not been conveyed to Doris for fear of exacerbating her precarious health. If deathbed visions are merely a hallucination, how is it possible for the dying to see the spirits of people they believe are still alive?

In Sir William's seminal study of such phenomena, *Death-Bed Visions*, published in 1926, he countered the accusation that the dying are hallucinating by pointing out that all of the subjects he studied were lucid and rational at the time. Moreover, the dying are frequently astounded by what they see because it does not conform to what they had been conditioned to see at the moment of death. For example, children spoke of angels without wings which in Catholic Ireland at that time was contrary to the archetypal image they were familiar with.

Thirty years later in New York City, parapsychologist Karlis Osis was inspired by Barrett's book to instigate a study of his own. Drawing on the experience of doctors and nurses, Osis was able to state categorically that deathbed visions were not influenced by drugs or the specifics of the individual's illness. Neither did they exhibit any characteristics peculiar to those experienced by the mentally ill or non-critical patients. Furthermore, only the terminally ill reported seeing people they knew to be dead and they were uncommonly coherent while they were describing what they had seen or were seeing at that moment.

In addition, other factors relating to social status, age, education and religion appeared to have no bearing on the nature or content of the visions.

In the 1970s Osis collaborated with Icelandic psychologist Erlendur Haraldsson on a more extensive study in which 1,708 patients in America and India were interviewed. The results concluded that the experience of patients on both continents was essentially the same, although the Americans tended to see deceased relatives waiting for them whereas the more religious Indian patients often told of seeing spiritual figures.

In 1977 Osis and Haraldsson compiled a book of their most compelling cases, published under the title *At the Hour of Death*, from which the following examples are taken.

A paramedic who comforted a dying 78-year-old man later reported that whenever the visions appeared the patient's chest pains subsided and a radiant smile appeared on his face. 'It was so beautiful, you just can't tell anyone,' he would say to the orderly, 'it was a breathtaking scene, more so than anything in life.'

The transformation was even more evident in the case of an elderly woman who had been described by her nurse as having been very mean prior to these visions. As she recalled:

> One night she called me to see how bright and lovely heaven is. Then she looked at me and seemed surprised: 'Oh, but you can't see it, you aren't here [in heaven], you are over there.' She became very peaceful and happy ... and she permitted her meanness to die ... I don't think these are hallucinations, they are ... very real.

What is significant is that even though the medical professionals and family members who are in attendance at the end can't share the patient's visions, they are nevertheless struck by the transformation in both the dying person and the ambience around them. The husband of Wilma Ashby who miraculously recovered after being visited by her dead twin brother Willard remarked that he felt he had been struck by lightning when he entered her hospital room. In another incident a nurse noted that the middle-aged woman she was attending was transformed by an unseen presence, which even the hardened medical professionals treating her could not fail to have sensed:

> ... her attitude seemed to have changed entirely. This was more than [just] a change of the [depressed] mood I had seen her in many times [before] ... It seemed as if there was something [here that was] just a little beyond us ... There was something which made us feel that ... she [had] some contact with the beyond and it had a happy effect on her.

Osis and Haraldsson concluded that these cases 'seem to support the hypothesis that death-bed visions are, in part, based on extrasensory perception of some form of external reality rather than having entirely subjective origins'.

## A new reality

Belief in an immortal soul has been a core concept of almost every culture since prehistoric times and continues to be so for the simple reason that soul travel is a universal experience and an increasingly common one. A recent Gallup Poll (1992) revealed that more than 11 million Americans claim to have had an OBE. That figure is likely to rise as life-saving medical technology and techniques mean that more people than ever before are being brought back from the brink of death, coupled with the fact that medical professionals are now aware of the phenomenon, even if they do not yet understand it and are unable to accept that it is a genuine subjective spiritual experience.

The American writer Ernest Hemingway was the personification of the hard-drinking, cigar-smoking, womanising macho male and the last person one would expect to admit to having had an out-of-body experience. But while serving as an officer with the US Ambulance Corps in the Italian campaign of 1918 the young Hemingway was struck in the leg by shrapnel from a mortar shell and felt his soul drawn out of his body as readily as '... you'd pull a silk handkerchief out of a pocket'. He flew around the battlefield for some minutes before returning and later drew on the experience for his wartime novel *A Farewell to Arms*. In the novel the hero Frederick Henry expands on the author's impressions, 'I went out swiftly, all of myself and I knew I was dead and that it had all been a mistake to think you just died.'

Another individual with no patience for flights of fancy was the aviator Charles Lindbergh, who made the first solo transatlantic flight in 1927. It took the all-American hero 50 years to pluck up the courage to admit that he had had an out-of-body experience in the final hours of that historic flight.

> *I existed independently of time and matter. I felt myself departing from my body as I imagine a spirit would depart ... But I remained connected to my body through a long extended strand, a strand so tenuous that it could have been severed by a breath ... My visions are easily explained away through reason, but the longer I live the more limited I believe rationality to be.*

# Raymond Moody

The term 'near-death experience' is a comparatively recent one and was coined by counsellor and doctor of philosophy Dr Raymond Moody. In 1965, Moody, then an unprepossessing 20-year-old philosophy student, attended a seminar at the University of Virginia that was to radically alter his entrenched belief in his own mortality and encourage millions more to consider the possibility of life after death. The theme under discussion was whether or not man possessed an immortal soul, the existence of which the great philosophers had argued eloquently for and against for centuries. The debate was stimulating but purely speculative until the professor mentioned that he knew of a local psychiatrist who claimed to have recently had a life-transforming out-of-body experience after being pronounced clinically dead. Dr George Ritchie had been successfully resuscitated after suffering a fatal bout of double pneumonia and on recovering described with great enthusiasm and awe his encounter with beings of light in another dimension.

A few months later Moody took the opportunity to hear Dr Ritchie tell his story to a group of students and was impressed by the psychiatrist's sincerity and the fact that a respected physician was prepared to speak publicly on the subject.

It wasn't until four years later, after Moody had qualified and was teaching philosophy himself, that he heard of a similar case from one of his own students which set him on the path that was to change his life. He began compiling a dossier of cases which he added to after entering medical school in 1972. By 1975 he had collected enough credible empirical evidence to publish his first book *Life After Life*. It became an instant international bestseller and although it wasn't the first book devoted to the phenomenon, it was the first to bring the subject to wide public awareness and introduce the term 'near-death experience'.

To Moody's surprise the descriptions he had gathered were uncannily consistent, suggesting that his patients had all shared the same experience, although they came from a wide variety of backgrounds and subscribed to different beliefs. Some had been firm disbelievers in the existence of life after death and yet they described very similar experiences and were clearly as profoundly affected as the others.

Dr Moody identified a number of common elements, which it appears have been shared by thousands of other individuals who have made similar claims in subsequent studies, although not every person has experienced these events in the same sequence. However, in almost every case the process of death was characterised by an absence of pain and an overwhelming sensation of serenity which allayed all fears at the moment of separation, even in cases of violent or sudden death. Many patients described the ecstasy they felt on finding themselves floating free of their physical body and watching as the doctors and nurses frantically attempted to revive them. Several recalled trying in vain to tell them not to bother, that they were happy to be rid of the burden of their sick or injured body, but nobody seemed aware of their presence. Curiously, the 'deceased' could hear everything that the medical team said during the crisis and were later able to repeat it. They were also able to describe precisely what had happened while they were technically 'dead', the details of which were subsequently verified by the hospital staff. Many spent what they later learnt had been several minutes out of the body, during which they were drawn down a long dark tunnel to emerge in a pastoral landscape where they were welcomed by deceased friends and relatives. There was an innate sense of familiarity about this place and a feeling of 'coming home'.

At some point in the journey the 'deceased' encounters a formless being of light which some are inclined on their return to interpret as God, Jesus or an angel, depending on their beliefs, although most have accepted it as being the embodiment of Love rather than an identifiable entity. From the light a voice asks if the individual is ready to die, which has the effect of reminding them of their responsibilities or of unfinished business on earth. This is usually sufficient to draw them back into their body with a firm determination not to waste another moment of their life. Some have spoken of being asked by the light what they have done in their life, although this was not said with any sense of judgement, after which they reviewed the events of their life in a series of flashbacks.

One interviewee in a later study described the process as:

> *a total reliving of every thought I had ever thought,*
> *every word I had ever spoken and every deed I had ever*
> *done; plus the effect of each thought, word and deed on*
> *everyone who had come within my environment or*
> *sphere of influence whether I knew them or not...*
>
> (P.M.H. Atwater *Coming back to Life* 1988)

Another described it as 'the most beautiful thing I had ever seen, and at the same time the most horrifying thing I was ever to experience'.

One young man found himself watching his life rewind in the company of a guide who he described as a father figure.

> *He seemed to ask me all the right questions at all the*
> *right times. I was able to pinpoint all of the things*
> *necessary to change myself.*
>
> (Kenneth Ring *Lessons from the Light*, 2000)

From the descriptions it sounds as if each person is judged by their own conscience, or higher self, rather than a celestial court, although some have recalled having to live through certain significant events once again, during which they have the perspective and feelings of those they have wronged in life.

## Reactionary reactions

Inevitably there were critics from the scientific establishment who dismissed NDEs as a figment of the dying brain or as a symptom of mental illness. Doctors voiced their reservations, arguing that thousands of patients had been resuscitated without claiming to have undergone the near-death experience. Sceptics observed that a few hundred anecdotal case histories do not qualify as a serious scientific study. But in the course of the next 20 years dozens of books appeared along with television documentaries, radio programmes, magazine and newspaper investigations citing thousands of well-documented cases recounted by people from every walk of life, background and belief, and even those who had vehemently denied the existence of an afterlife, all of whom shared strikingly similar experiences. The evidence was overwhelming and had it been in support of another phenomenon scientists would have been forced to concede it to be fact. But the existence of the soul is unverifiable from a scientific point of view and the near-death experience is a subjective one that can only be experienced and not measured or recorded. Nevertheless, serious scientific studies were established into related phenomena such as lucid dreams and remote viewing and these have added to our understanding of the nature of human consciousness.

With the publication of Moody's research the cynical arguments of rationalist philosophers such as the eighteenth-century Scot, David Hume, were rendered redundant. Hume had declared belief in an afterlife as irrational and asked, 'By what arguments or analogies can we prove any state of existence which no one ever saw, and which no way resembles any that ever was seen?' Well, now we have hundreds of thousands of personal accounts, which it would be irrational to deny.

The most common argument against the validity of the near-death experience is that it is a hallucination created by a brain starved of oxygen or a lucid dream triggered by the release of endorphins (the body's natural painkillers) or as a side effect of prescribed drugs administered in the hospital. But such desperate theories do not explain the many instances in which the patient is able to report details of the medical procedures used to revive them or the personnel who were present. In some cases the patient even managed to visit their relatives who were waiting anxiously nearby.

On being revived one lady complained to her maid that she shouldn't have brought her daughter to the hospital in clothes that didn't match, although she hadn't yet seen the little girl, still sitting patiently in the reception area out of sight of her mother.

More remarkable was the case Dr Moody cited of an elderly patient who was unconscious when he ordered a nurse to go and fetch crucial medication. Normally the nurse would have broken the top of the glass vial containing the medicine with a paper towel to avoid the risk of cutting herself. But in this case it was an emergency, so the nurse cracked the top off with her unprotected fingers and then rushed back to hand it to Dr Moody. Even if the patient had been conscious she would not have seen how the nurse opened the vial. But as soon as she recovered she turned to the nurse and admonished her for breaking the glass with her bare hands. She had witnessed the action as she hovered over the nurse in the next room. Such cases are surprisingly common.

But perhaps the most compelling evidence of all was obtained by Professor Kenneth Ring in his 1996 study *Mindsight: Near-Death and Out-Of-Body Experiences in the Blind.* Fourteen of Ring's subjects had been blind from birth yet they described their NDEs in identical terms to those reported by sighted persons. According to Ring one interviewee, Vicki Umipeg, could not even understand the concept of light because her optic nerves had been destroyed shortly after birth and yet she was able to describe the scene of an accident in which she had been involved in considerable detail, and the subsequent efforts made to revive her while she observed from outside her body. All she said was confirmed.

# Empathic NDEs

Moody himself experienced a rare phenomenon during the last moments of his mother's life. He was at his mother's bedside together with his wife, his brother-in law and his two sisters. As his mother took her last breaths they all sensed that the room was swirling and that they were lifted up an inch or so by an influx of collective energy. One of the sisters saw their father who had died two years earlier standing by the bed and at that moment Moody's brother-in-law, a Methodist minister, cried out 'Can you feel it?' as the atmosphere became charged. Not one to let an opportunity pass, Moody investigated such phenomena and discovered that empathic NDEs (which involve the witness sharing vicariously in the transition experience or becoming aware of a change in the quality of energy in the immediate area) are comparatively common among care workers, hospice nurses and relatives who are present at the moment of death. These phenomena were unknown a few decades ago simply because relatives were usually ushered from the room when the end was coming and the terminally ill were not given the level of personal care and attention that they are today. Such experiences also invalidate the argument that NDEs are a biochemical hallucination in the dying brain, because the witnesses who share the experience are alert and aware of the phenomenon.

## The convert

One of Moody's most esteemed converts was Atlanta cardiologist Michael B. Sabom, a hardened sceptic who had initially scoffed at Moody's claims during an adult Sunday School debate.

In a 1979 article on the subject for the *Journal of the American Medical Association* Sabom had declared:

> *People who undergo these 'death experiences' are suffering from a hypoxic [oxygen-starved] state, during which they try to deal psychologically with the anxieties provoked by medical procedures and talk ... We are dealing here with the fantasy of death.*

But after interviewing one of his own patients in preparation for a presentation before a churchwide audience, Sabom's reservations crumbled away:

> *To my utter amazement the details matched the descriptions in* Life After Life. *I was even more impressed by her sincerity and the deep personal significance her experience had had for her.*

Five years later he had published the results of his own exhaustive study into the subject and was forced to admit:

> *I am convinced that my original suspicions about this were wrong.*

## Celebrity NDEs

Hollywood celebrities helped to increase public awareness and acceptance of the paranormal during the 1970s and 80s. They were led by celebrity psychic Uri Geller and actress Shirley Maclaine, who went on to write several bestsellers based on her personal experiences. But other well-known personalities had shared similar experiences, although they were reluctant to speak openly of them at the time.

In 1964 comic actor Peter Sellers suffered the first in a series of heart attacks and was declared clinically dead. He later recalled:

> *I just floated out of my physical form and I saw them
> cart my body away to the hospital. I went with it ... I
> wasn't frightened ... I was fine ... it was my body that
> was in trouble.*

Sellers was strangely indifferent to the frantic efforts being made to
revive him:

> *I saw an incredibly beautiful, bright, loving white light
> above me. I wanted to go to that white light more than
> anything. I've never wanted anything more. I know
> there was love, real love, on the other side of the light
> which was attracting me so much. It was kind and
> loving and I remember thinking, 'That's God'.*

But try as he might the light remained out of reach.

> *Then I saw a hand reach through the light. I tried to
> touch it, to grab onto it, to clasp it so it could sweep me
> up and pull me through it.*

At that moment he heard a voice say:

> *'It's not time. Go back and finish. It's not time'.*

Sellers returned to his body as his heart restarted, but he was haunted
by the memory of that elusive bliss for the remainder of his life. He lost his
fear of death and became less restless and more reflective, which unnerved
his wife Britt Ekland. The experience also gave him the idea that his talent
for mimicry might have derived from unconscious memories of past lives
and a connection with the characters he might have been. He confided to
friend Shirley MacLaine:

> *I know I have lived many times before ... that
> experience confirmed it to me, because in this lifetime I
> felt what it was for my soul to actually be out of my
> body. But ever since I came back, I don't know why I
> don't know what it is I'm supposed to do, or what I
> came back for.*

American TV actor Robert Pastorelli was taken to intensive care with
critical injuries after being involved in a car accident at the age of nineteen.

> *I was in excruciating pain. Then, in the next second,
> there was no pain ... I was floating above myself,
> looking down at my unconscious body lying in the
> hospital emergency room with my eyes closed ... I*

> *thought, 'Well, this must be death.' I even saw a priest*
> *giving me the last rites. But it was the most peaceful*
> *feeling in the world. Then I saw my father starting to*
> *faint out of grief ... When I looked down and saw my*
> *father's pain it had an effect on me. I firmly believe that*
> *at that moment I made a decision to live, not die. The*
> *next thing I knew I was waking up back in my body.*

During an interview with talk show host Larry King, British-born actress Elizabeth Taylor recalled her experience of passing through a tunnel towards a brilliant white light after dying during surgery. She described being reunited with her third husband Michael Todd, whom she considered to be the great love of her life. He had been killed in a plane crash in 1958. But although she wanted to stay with him in this blissful state he told her that she had to return, at which point she snapped back into her body.

> *I find it hard to talk about because it sounds so corny;*
> *they had given me up for dead and put my death notice*
> *on the wall. I shared this with the people that were in*
> *the room next to me. Then after that I told another*
> *group of friends, and I thought, 'Wow, this sounds*
> *really screwy. I think I'd better keep quiet about this.'*

> *For a long time I didn't talk about it, and it's still hard*
> *for me to talk about. But I have shared it with people*
> *with AIDS because if the moment occurs and you're*
> *really sharing, it's real. I am not afraid of death,*
> *because I have been there.*

Screen actor Donald Sutherland shared the memory of his near-death experience which occurred in 1979. He had reached a crisis in his battle with meningitis when:

> *... the pain, fever and acute distress seemed to*
> *evaporate. I was floating above my body, surrounded*
> *by soft blue light. I began to glide down a long tunnel,*
> *away from the bed ... but suddenly I found myself back*
> *in my body. The doctors told me later that I had*
> *actually died for a time.*

*Dallas* actor Larry Hagman's NDE in 1995 brought him self-insight and the realisation that death is

> *just another stage of our development and that we go*
> *on to different levels of existence ... This was not the*
> *end. There were more levels, an infinite number of*

*levels, of existence, each one adding to the hum of the
cosmic orchestra, as if we're always spiralling upward
until we reach a state of atomic bliss ...*

Other celebrities who have had NDEs include comedian Chevy Chase, actress Sharon Stone, singer Tony Bennett, Burt Reynolds and *CSI* star William Petersen, who compared his experience to that of the lead character in the musical *All That Jazz*.

## The twilight zone

Not all NDEs involve an unscheduled visit to heaven.

The Connecticut psychologist Kenneth Ring records a very curious episode in his scrupulously scientific study *Life at Death* (1980).

The subject, who wished to remain anonymous, was born in England but later moved to the US. At the age of ten, while he was still living in England, he had a near-death experience in which he looked through the eyes of his future adult self at his children who were playing in the living room of their home in America. At this point in his life the subject had not even visited the States, nor did he have any reason to believe that he would live there in the future.

The NDE occurred in 1941 during an operation for a burst appendix. When the subject recovered he was troubled by very specific 'memories' of the future that he couldn't account for. He 'knew' that he would be married when he was 28, that he would have two children and live in the house that he had 'seen' in his vision. Perhaps the most puzzling aspect was the fact that he knew what it felt like to be married although at the age of ten he admitted he couldn't conceive of that situation. It was this inexplicable sense of being a mature adult that nagged at him for the next 27 years.

In the vision he could see in front of him and to the right, but not to the left where he knew that his wife was sitting, which suggests that he was not permitted to in case this affected his future decisions and actions. If he had seen the girl he might not have felt it worthwhile to enter into a relationship with anyone else until he met her, which might have prevented him from meeting his future wife if she had a connection with the other girl. Odder still is the fact that in the vision one of the two children was a boy, but the subject went on to have two girls. The final piece of the puzzle is quite unsettling in its implications. Before he returned to consciousness the subject sensed that there was something inexplicable behind the facing wall, something that he simply couldn't understand. It was only when he realised that he was living through that 'memory' 27 years later in America with his children playing at his feet that he realised what the mysterious object was on the other side of the wall. It was a forced-air heater, and this type of heater was unknown in England when he had the vision in 1941.

Such experiences raise the question of what is the true nature of consciousness and the possibility that we have the latent ability to project awareness beyond the confines of the brain to other locations and perhaps even to other dimensions.

Ring concluded his extensive series of interviews by stating 'with considerable intellectual reluctance' that he attributed such phenomena to the existence of a 'higher self' and that it is this aspect of ourselves which survives death.

> *If one can accept the idea of a Higher Self it is not difficult to assume that that self – as well as the individual himself – is actually an aspect of God, or the Creator, or any term with which one feels comfortable.*

And despite being a man who put more faith in statistics than he did in anecdotal evidence, he had been persuaded

> *... that we continue to have a conscious existence after our physical death and that the core experience does represent its beginning, a glimpse of things to come. ... it is possible to become conscious of 'other realities' and that the coming close to death represents one avenue to a higher 'frequency domain' or reality, which will be fully accessible to us following what we call death ... Obviously, the thousands of NDErs who have been interviewed are speaking for millions of their silent brethren.*

## Scientific proof

Experiential evidence, compelling though it might be, is not conclusive proof of the existence of the etheric body, but there have been several persuasive scientific experiments which produced results that would be hard to contest.

The invention of the electroencephalograph (EEG) for recording electrical activity in the brain proved a major asset to paranormal research. The first occasion it was used to measure the brainwaves in an OBE experiment it produced patterns which Dr William Dement, a leading authority on sleep patterns, declared himself unable to identify. The subject, a Miss Z, had volunteered to have herself wired up to the EEG machine at the University of California under the supervision of psychologist Dr Charles Tart. Tart had a shelf built near the ceiling, out of eyesight, on which he placed a clock and a five-digit number chosen at random. On the fourth night of the experiment Miss Z produced the uncharacteristic brainwave patterns which Dement was later unable to identify and after she awoke gave Dr Tart the five-digit number she had seen while out of her body and the time she had seen on the clock, which coincided with the time of the unusual brain activity. It was beyond the laws of probability for her to have correctly guessed the five-digit number. There could be only one explanation for her success.

In the mid-1970s Dr Karlis Osis, Director of Research at the American Society for Psychical Research, designed a contraption for measuring disturbance in an electrical field. He then invited the well-known psychic Pat Price, a former California Police Commissioner, to enter the box in which the electrical field was being generated in his astral body to determine if it was possible to detect the presence of a person in their non-corporeal form. Price duly obliged and the data recorder went 'wild'. In a variation on this experiment Price and another psychic, Alex Tanous, were challenged to move a feather suspended on a string in an airtight enclosure. Again, Price and his colleagues proved their invisible presence in the room by agitating the feather, whose movements were recorded on graph paper in a similar way to a lie-detector test.

Tanous was equally obliging when asked to project into a totally black room so that the subtle radiance of his astral body could be measured. A number of acutely sensitive light sensors known as photomultipliers recorded a series of bursts of light at the very moment Tanous had claimed he would be in the sealed room.

The test was later replicated with animals which were known to be highly receptive to danger, a cat and a snake. Both were kept in separate cages and observed to establish their normal behaviour patterns while in captivity. Under the supervision of psychologist Dr Robert Morris of the Psychical Research Foundation in Durham, North Carolina, psychic Stuart Harary projected his astral body into each cage while Dr Morris recorded the animal's reactions. Both reacted violently. Researcher Scott Rogo noted that the snake stopped its routine circuit of the cage and became poised to attack the unseen presence. For 20 seconds it snapped at the air at exactly the same time that Harary said he was in the cage.

In addition to these and other convincing studies neuroscientists have recently discovered that consciousness leaves a dying person through the fourth ventricle of the brain, which is the first internal structure to form in the human embryo. It suggests that death is a natural and logical reversal of the process of birth and that consciousness returns the way it came. It is surely significant that at the moment consciousness leaves the brain the body loses between one quarter and three quarters of an ounce in weight, yet there is no loss of physical matter to account for this discrepancy.

# 6

# Glimpses of Heaven

Shakespeare may have been England's greatest dramatist and poet but he was wrong when he described heaven as the undiscovered country from which no traveller returns. Many thousands, perhaps hundreds of thousands of people have returned, bringing back descriptions of a pastoral paradise that are so strikingly similar that it must have a basis in reality even if it is not reality as we understand it.

One of the most detailed descriptions of the heavenly dimension was related to American psychic researcher David Wheeler by a man who suffered a fatal heart attack shortly after being admitted to hospital. The doctor who revived the patient, known only as Kenneth G, later admitted that he would not normally have attempted recovery but for the fact that he knew the man's daughter and felt obliged to do all he could. 'He was as dead as anyone I have ever seen,' recalled the doctor, who had observed signs of rigor mortis. 'I saw no real hope, but decided to go ahead as though there was.'

Kenneth G. survived his visit to the 'other side' with no physical ill-effects or brain damage, although conventional medical wisdom states that it is impossible to make a full recovery if the patient is clinically brain dead, as Kenneth G appears to have been. More extraordinary still was his experience of life in the world beyond.

He described a luxuriant landscape of verdant hills and valleys whose beauty was beyond comparison with anywhere on earth. He had the sensation of drifting gently down to land in a meadow of tall, waist-high grass which appeared to have no end. In the distance were dense forests, animals and an abundance of exotic flowers, the like of which he had never seen before.

He stood for some time taking in the majesty of his surroundings and listening to the grass rustling in the breeze. Then he heard a faint voice that he recognised as being that of his father who had died ten years before.

> 'What is he doing here', I thought to myself ... 'I don't
> know where I am, and my dead father is calling to me.'

*I accepted things as they were – what else could I do?*
*The voice kept faintly telling me, 'Kenneth, don't be*
*afraid. Do not worry, I have come to help you with your*
*journey. Don't be afraid of this. I've helped others.'*

The next moment he caught the sound of laughter and saw children playing in what appeared to be an amusement park in the distance. It reminded him of Coney Island which he had visited as a child. His wish to see the children brought him to them in the instant it took to form the thought.

*... all my old playmates were there, just like they were*
*sixty years ago ... None of them noticed me; they*
*continued to play in the amusement park as we had*
*done half a century ago ... I was a little boy again,*
*reliving [my] youth ... God, it was beautiful!*

*Death seemed to have blended the hereafter with the*
*fondest memories I carried through life. I know I went to*
*heaven with my most cherished childhood memories ...*
*How wrong it was for them to bring me back from such*
*a wonderful ... place.*

Those who have journeyed to the boundary between the worlds, to the periphery of Shakespeare's 'undiscovered country' describe it in remarkably similar terms.

Dr R.B. Hout, who recalled his impressions in *The Phenomena of Astral Projection*, compiled by Sylvan Muldoon and Hereward Carrington, was struck by its likeness to a natural environment such as that found in a grove or park, though it seemed to extend as far as the eye could see. On being reunited with his deceased mother Dr Hout observed:

*My being fairly blended with hers, and this moment*
*seemed the supreme happiness of my existence.*

He was overjoyed at seeing her so radiantly healthy

*... in the glory of her ... spirit body, free and attuned to*
*the plane of life upon which she was living.*

And Dr Hout was adamant that he was not confusing the vision with an unusually vivid dream.

*I would like to emphasize that these out-of-body*
*experiences are real to me, objective and tangible,*
*wherein I meet people living in a real world.*

71

One of Moody's interviewees recalled encounters with other discarnate souls and the sense their presence gave him.

> They were all people I had known in my past life, but who had passed on before ... They all seemed pleased. It was a very happy occasion and I felt that they had come to protect or to guide me. It was almost as if I were coming home, and they were there to greet or to welcome me.

Cultural anthropologist Patrick Gallagher had a similar experience in 1976 while lying in a coma following a serious car crash during which he experienced not one but several NDEs. Freed from his body he felt transformed and rose into the air where he found himself at the entrance to a tunnel.

> I saw a circular light in the distance ... of yellow-orange colour of total beauty ... When I left the tunnel, I entered a dazzlingly beautiful area ... It was complete space, that is ... totally and perfectly illuminated ... I saw [there] a number of people, some of whom were clothed and some of whom weren't. The clothing, which seemed transparent, was adornment but not ... shielding ...

> The people themselves [were] also of graceful beauty... Everyone there, as I knew the very moment I was there, seemed to possess a knowledge as radiant, transfiguring and ideal as the luminous light. And I possessed it, too... I knew that all one had to do was approach an interesting person and quite easily and almost immediately understand his essence. To do so completely required only a brief glance into the person's eyes without any speech ... the result was [a] consummate exchange of knowledge ... Without reflection or words, I knew them as completely as they knew me, and finally understood why poets cite eyes as entrance to the soul ... I also knew that the illuminating light would never cease ... I also understood that everyone present was in a state of perfect compassion with everyone else and everything else... These ideal conditions produced a phenomenal state, for neither hate nor any other disturbing passion was present – only the total presence of love ...

Gallagher described it as being the sum of all that he ever wanted to know or to be, but he knew that he had to return and that by doing so he would 'lose all but a splinter' of his luminous knowledge.

## A garden in the stars

In the autumn of 1968 in a small town in India a Doctor Kahn was treating his critically ill two-and-a-half-year-old daughter, Durdana, who he feared was close to death, when she suddenly and miraculously revived. In fact, she had been clinically dead for fifteen minutes. On opening her eyes she described how she had travelled to a beautiful garden 'in the stars' through which flowed four coloured streams. This was no earthly garden for there was no sun in the sky and the plants were translucent, glowing from the life force within.

The toddler was not alone in paradise. Her grandfather, who had died some years before, had been there to greet her together with an older woman whom the child did not recognise, although she had a strong resemblance to her own mother.

Durdana wanted to stay but at this point she heard her father calling for her to return which prompted her grandfather to say that they would have to ask God if she could leave. Curiously, for a child who had been brought up in a devout Hindu household, Durdana did not describe God in Hindu terms but as an amorphous radiant blue light from which a voice issued, asking if she wanted to return. She replied that she had to go because her father was calling and with that she drifted back into her body.

Despite her father's medical background he was convinced that her vision had not been a delusion brought on by her fever. The first reason was that she had described awakening in her father's bed, but in her delirious state she could not have known it was his. She had been expressly forbidden to play in his bed and would have expected to have been carried to her own bed or her mother's when she needed comforting. The only way she could have known that it was her father's bed was if she had indeed seen herself lying there as she returned to her body. The second reason he was convinced that she was telling the truth was that she was later able to identify her great grandmother's photograph, which she had never seen. Her parents did not possess any pictures of the old lady who had died before Durdana was born. The only copy was in her uncle's house and she had never visited the house prior to that day.

There is an intriguing footnote to the story. Twelve years later, after the family had moved to England, Durdana and her father appeared on British television to contribute to a debate on the subject of life after death. Durdana brought along some of the paintings she had made of the celestial garden to illustrate her story. The experience had evidently left a lasting impression on her and a need to express in her art her desire to return to the garden.

The following day an excited viewer contacted the family to say that she had visited the very same place during one of her own near-death experiences and was able to describe other details which Durdana had omitted from her paintings.

'I nearly jumped out of my chair when I saw this picture on the television,' said Mrs Goldsmith who, it transpired, was one of Dr Kahn's patients.

Admittedly, it sounds suspicious that of all the people to have shared this experience it was someone who knew Dr Kahn, but it was precisely because she knew him that Mrs Goldsmith felt confident to contact him and share her experience. There may have been many other people watching the programme who recognised the environment depicted in the painting, but if there were any, they evidently preferred to keep it to themselves. Of course we only have the older woman's word that she saw more than the little girl, but when they met, Durdana and Mrs Goldsmith talked animatedly for some considerable time and agreed on many details which neither had spoken of before and which were not included in the girl's picture.

This account is all the more remarkable because at the time of her NDE Durdana was too young to have been influenced or conditioned by her parent's beliefs which, in any case, would not have conformed to this particular image of heaven.

Compare the description of the heavenly garden given by Durdana with the following NDE recorded by a 55-year-old man who recalled the scene as vividly as when he had first seen it, 45 years before, following an adverse reaction to penicillin.

> Black clouds swirled all around me like I was in a heavy fog. Then suddenly, a point of light appeared. It moved closer and closer to me until the clouds suddenly cleared, and I was standing next to a narrow stream. I began to walk next to the stream until it got so narrow that I could step over it.
>
> The other side of the stream was extremely peaceful. There were hills on the peaceful side that were lighted from behind and looked beautiful.
>
> As I walked, I was approached by an old man with a beard. I don't know for sure who he was, but I have the feeling he was one of my grandfathers. He stopped me and told me to go back across the stream. 'It's not your time', he said.

*I turned and looked at the stream. It was quite wide at
this point, but it soon narrowed. Then I simply crossed
and passed into my body.*

(Melvin Morse, *Closer to the Light* 1991)

If in this case the imagery is merely an externalisation of the boy's
feelings, the fog would symbolise his confusion and the stream the point of
no return, while the old man could be seen as a personification of his
internal parent (the superego) or the archetypal wise teacher, depending on
whether you subscribe to Freud or Jung.

The other explanation is that it is an alternative reality (in the sense
that a dream is real while we are dreaming it) and that the boy's intuition
was correct in assuming the old man to be his deceased grandfather who
he had never met but recognised in the empathic world of spirit.

Those who would claim that NDEs are self-fulfilling fantasies created
by people who see only what they have been conditioned or expect to see
should note that this argument is contradicted by the evidence. As one lady
remarked:

*What I experienced challenged everything I have ever
read, seen or heard, everything I believed ... I've tried to
tell myself it was a dream, but I know in my heart it
wasn't.*

## Experience

Not all NDEs involve the individual passing through a tunnel of light, or
encountering the common features identified by Raymond Moody, but even
these atypical cases appear to confirm that the afterlife is a state of being
and not a state of mind. Significantly, religious beliefs and expectations
play no part in determining the quality or nature of such experiences.

Seventy-six-year-old Bert Kovus of Margate in Kent was and remains a
committed Christian who believed in an afterlife of some kind, but admits
that he used to dismiss people who claimed to have had NDEs as highly
imaginative – until he had an experience of his own.

*I had been admitted to an Intensive Care unit suffering
from multiple organ failure where I lay drifting in and
out of consciousness for eleven days. Then at one point
I became acutely aware that I was out of my body in an
area that was totally fluorescent white. I had no sense of
spatial dimensions or of standing on solid ground. I was
either in it or part of it, whatever 'it' was. It wasn't a
place as we know it. It was not a physical space. There*

*was no floor, no walls. It was a world beyond the senses. Another reality. It cannot be described in words except to say that it was a place of total, utter peace. It was so all-pervasive that I felt I shouldn't even disturb it with a thought.*

*I was not conscious of my body but I was observing from a point of view as if I was standing. Then I heard a genderless voice say, 'He's got to go back', and looking upward I saw two white-robed figures lying on their sides, one on either side. The other asked why and the first one answered, 'There is something he is yet to do.' At that moment I hoped they would say what it was. I was still my curious, impatient self and was really disappointed when I didn't hear the answer. Instead they started to drift upward away from me to converge at a point in the far distance. In fact I remember thinking, 'If they go this slowly its going to take them months to meet at the top.' But on and upward they went. When they finally disappeared I opened my eyes and saw the dirtiest, ugliest thing I had ever seen. It was the dirt on the ceiling of the Intensive Care ward, which I saw nothing wrong with when I looked at it the next day, but having come from that place of perfection and peace, this physical world offended my sight. The doctor then leaned over me and said that he was glad I was back with the living or something like that because they had just managed to revive me. But I was left with an overwhelming sense of disappointment that I hadn't been able to go on to the next level and instead had to come back here.*

*Now I can understand why psychics and mediums don't get anything meaningful from their communications with the dead. The dead exist in a place that is so remote from this physical reality that they couldn't possibly return even with a great effort of will. And they wouldn't want to see this world again. Once you have experienced that sublime peace you simply don't want to know anything else. You are liberated from life's cares and the crudity and density of physical existence.*

*I am the last person I expected this to happen to and I'm a better person for it.*

*I know without a doubt that what I experienced was real. It changed my attitude to life completely. I used to be short-tempered, intense and cynical, but now I am easy-going and optimistic and I have lost my fear of death. But having been out of this world doesn't mean that I think that what happens in life isn't important. In fact, it has left me with the feeling that we shouldn't waste one moment of our time on earth or take the blessing of life for granted.*

# After-effects

It is a popular misconception that NDEs transform the individual into a vegetarian New Age tree-hugger. It is true that most of the people who return from their brush with death do so with a renewed determination to make the most of their second chance, but they do not become docile or eager to embrace death. They simply lose their dread of dying and are less intense, intolerant and impatient towards others. Sometimes their laid-back attitude can infuriate their partners and families who had become used to their curmudgeonly self-centred ways. And though it is always a profoundly spiritual experience it does not necessarily lead to them disowning their religious beliefs. Dr Raymond Moody cites the case of a Methodist minister who regularly threatened his congregation with the prospect of hell and damnation, but who afterwards preached the value of compassion and forgiveness. He claimed to have been shown the error of his ways by a being of light, who pointed out that he was making his parishioners guilty and fearful. According to Dr Melvin Morse of the Children's Orthopedic Hospital in Seattle, religious beliefs do not influence the experience, only the individual's interpretation of it. After an NDE both believers and non-believers alike agree that they have no interest in the dogmatic aspect of religion and its empty rituals. For them the heart of a religion should be how to cultivate compassion and live a more spiritual life. More significantly, Dr Morse – who monitored his patients periodically for more than 20 years after their initial interview – concluded that the positive effects of an NDE remain undiminished even after such a prolonged period. The sense of having shared something sacred remains, despite the influence of the negative people around them and the tragic events with which they are continually bombarded in the nightly news.

Clinicians who have studied the phenomenon are in agreement that all the people they have interviewed are more content and positive now than they were prior to their experience, although they are acutely aware of their own mortality and of the comparatively short time they have on earth to accomplish whatever might be the purpose of this latest incarnation.

# Heaven and hell

If there is a heaven, are we to believe that there is also a hell? It is my understanding that heaven is a state of being, whereas hell is simply a state of mind, a self-inflicted form of torment created out of guilt or a severe addiction to our baser instincts, or substances such as alcohol and narcotics. The mere belief that one is going to hell, or even the fear of that possibility, does not appear to be sufficient to create that reality as even the most self-centred and fearful people who claim to have had NDEs share the same bliss, suggesting that we leave behind our fears when we become detached from our physical body.

The hell described in Hindu, Buddhist and other ancient sacred texts is clearly mythological, an attempt to explain the darker side of human nature by sketching a symbolic landscape of our fears so that we are forced to come face to face with our own shadows. In contrast, the traditional Christian hell with its horned devil and demons is largely a creation of the medieval mind, devised to frighten the potential sinner into keeping in line and attending church on a regular basis. The early Church leaders knew that if they relied solely on the faithful and pure in heart their churches would be empty. Like modern movie-makers they knew the value of a good scare and how the devil could bring the punters in, to put it crudely. Fear is more effective than faith. The promise of paradise was not sufficient to ensure commitment; there also had to be the fear of eternal damnation to encourage correct conduct and generous donations. It was a matter of simple psychology – the carrot and the stick.

Whilst there are literally hundreds of thousands of recorded accounts of positive near-death experiences, there are comparatively few examples on record of negative experiences and these are highly subjective, differing in detail from one another and therefore largely suggestive of a particular state of mind rather than a state of being. From the descriptions they appear to be indicative of conditions of depression or of nightmare.

One woman would say no more than, 'If you leave here a tormented soul, you will be a tormented soul over there too,' while a widower who had attempted suicide in his despair said cryptically, 'I didn't go where [my wife] was. I went to an awful place ... I immediately saw what a mistake I had made.' The realisation was evidently enough to snap him back to waking consciousness.

Recent research into negative NDEs by Tony Lawrence, a lecturer in psychology at Coventry University, and others has concluded that they usually involve what Lawrence calls 'an absence of experience' or a feeling of being dragged down into a pit. Both sound more like a nightmare in which a sensation of helplessness, disorientation and despair manifests as disturbing images and emotions, rather than a real experience, for they have none of the substance or detail of the positive NDE experience. It would seem that negative NDEs are the manifestation of a process of inner purification or a fear of annihilation.

As the eighteenth-century Swedish mystic Emanuel Swedenborg noted in *Heaven and Hell*, certain individuals may be so unprepared for the new reality that 'they begin to feel pain and to be so tormented within that they feel as though they were in hell rather than in heaven'.

## Describing heaven

*No eye can hear, no ear can see, no mind can comprehend*
*what heaven is like.*

(Rabbi Yochanan ben Zachai)

The question which has preoccupied and frustrated mystics through the centuries is not whether heaven exists, but how to describe the indescribable, a state of being which is beyond our comprehension and the ability of language to convey.

The predicament is summed up in the story of the turtle and the fish which is said to have originated with the Buddha but will also be familiar to Muslims and Jews.

A turtle and a fish were basking in the shallows of the sea and wondering what it must be like to live on dry land. After some time, the fish asked the turtle to explore the beach and find out. Reluctantly the turtle agreed and after some time returned, but was only able to say that the fine white sun-baked sand on the beach was not like the wet sand on the sea bed, that the vegetation did not feel like seaweed and that walking in the open air was not like swimming in the sea. The fish was naturally frustrated and demanded to know what it was like to live on the land, but the turtle insisted that there was nothing in their experience that he could relate it to.

The thirteenth-century Italian theologian St Thomas Aquinas faced a similar dilemma. St Thomas devoted his life to contemplation of the divine but after he had a momentary glimpse of God he found words inadequate to describe his experience and refused even to speak of it. After months spent in silent reverie trying to recapture that elusive moment, he was asked by his publisher to complete the manuscript of his masterwork, the *Summa Theologiae*, whereupon St Thomas declared it to be redundant in the light of what had been revealed to him in that one brief instant.

# The view from heaven

Perhaps the strongest argument against the existence of heaven as the summerland of eternal rest and sensual indulgence is that, if we have all been there before, why can we not remember it? Even under hypnotic regression subjects who have been forthcoming with details regarding their previous incarnations become inexplicably reticent in talking of the state between lives, except in the most vague terms.

After reading innumerable accounts of near-death experiences and having experienced altered states of consciousness myself it is my contention that we do not remember because heaven does not exist as an objective reality, but as a euphoric state of awareness, and therefore cannot be re-created using the mental faculty of memory. It is something we have experienced, not a place we have visited. It is a subjective experience which we can share to a degree, in the same way that hundreds of people can listen to a concert, but take away different impressions of the performance. In the case of heaven they describe a pastoral paradise but differ as to specific details. And the being of light who is present in all NDEs is subsequently understood as having been either God, Jesus, an angel or an amorphous benign energy. Why? Because they each interpreted the same experience according to their own personal expectations or perceptions. But that does not invalidate the reality of the experience, only their interpretation of it. A suitable analogy might be the way different critics will look at a painting. One might be overwhelmed by the artist's use of symmetry, colour, perspective and so on. Another might see only a two-dimensional canvas daubed with blobs of paint. A third might be amused by what the artist is saying about the object or incident he is portraying while yet another may be offended by the intellectual conceit. And when they have left the gallery even the most eloquent critic will not be able to convey the sense of what the painting looks like, other than to draw comparison with other works or contextualise it as relating to a specific school or period.

The same dilemma confronts the music critic or even the person attempting to describe their holiday to a friend. We talk in generalities and clichés even about experiences that mean so much to us, so why should it be any different on the other side? How many times have we heard people on the news describe the loss of a loved one as 'devastating'? And who can describe a so-called peak experience, such as winning several million on the lottery, seeing their child smile or even sexual ecstasy, in adequate language so that someone who has not experienced it will understand exactly what they mean? We simply do not have satisfactory expressions to convey our most profound feelings, so how can we be expected to convey the transcendent bliss of the afterlife in other than generic terms?

Perhaps only poets can come close and even they can only give an impression of what they are describing. If heaven is indeed a dreamlike dimension where we exist in our emotional body then it is to be expected that we will describe it in emotional terms.

As the American writer Kurt Leland remarked at the end of his weighty study of the subject, *The Unanswered Question*, it is not a question of what we will see but how we will see it.

## A spirit companion

And what of the worlds beyond heaven? The following story offers a glimpse of what may lie ahead for us as well as reaffirming that death is only a temporary separation from those we love.

In her autobiographical account *Beyond the Boundary of Life and Death*, Dutch psychologist Elleke van Kraalingen describes how she became aware of the spirit of her fiancé, Hermod, whose death she had witnessed only moments before when he was struck by a speeding car on a dirt road in Jamaica. Hermod, a Norwegian doctor, appears to have had a vague presentiment of his own death in the days before the fatal accident, but instead of unsettling him, it gave him a sense of his life having come full circle. After years of frustration and struggle in his private and professional life he had come to accept life as he found it, instead of bemoaning what he had previously perceived as the random cruelty and endemic injustice of this world. He told Elleke that her love had helped him to surrender to fate and that if he should die at that moment he would consider himself fulfilled. As he said this, Elleke sensed a 'radiance' around him. Moments later he was struck by a speeding car and almost immediately lost consciousness. As she knelt over him Elleke sensed a 'tearing apart' as if the psychic bond between them was violently separated. Then she saw his soul leave his body in the form of a mist and sensed his presence standing behind her while she made frantic efforts to revive him. Although part of her was in shock, another part sensed an enfolding light bringing her comfort and a sense of serenity. When Elleke walked back to their hotel she felt Hermod walking beside her with his hand in hers.

Later in the book she describes how he materialised in their room. Being a psychologist she instinctively tried to explain the image away as a hallucination created by grief and the need to believe that their love would last beyond this lifetime. She covered her eyes and told herself that it was only her imagination, but when she looked again he was still there, sitting on the end of the bed. It was then that she heard his voice inside her mind, insistent but compassionate. 'I'm still here,' he assured her. 'There is no

81

death, there is no time, there's only reality.' Again, there was a radiance around him and this time she sensed the presence of other unseen beings providing him with support.

When he had gone Elleke wrote down all that she could remember so that she could answer her own doubts when they came. She had no reason to believe that she would experience such a phenomenon again, but the next day he reappeared to accompany her through the painful process of identifying his body and giving statements to the police. He remained by her side for four days altogether until after the funeral. Then she was left alone in the apartment they had shared.

To centre herself and restore some sense of normality Elleke began to meditate, but as soon as she attained a deep sense of relaxation he appeared again and with a tug pulled her out of her body. She too was now a body of light looking back at her physical self sitting crossed-legged on the floor far below. Though she now existed in a non-physical state she felt this was more real than the physical world which she could still see around them. She was now more alive than ever and felt a vibrancy she had never experienced before. They embraced, but she soon felt drained of energy, 'lost focus', as she described it, and went back into her body.

Over the next six months he reappeared each day to invite her to accompany him into other realms of higher consciousness. But each time it was at his choosing. Whenever she willed it to happen, nothing occurred.

She describes the first dimension as a translucent world of vivid colours inhabited by beings that she perceived as shapes without physical substance. They were of a more 'elevated consciousness' but they were not angels as we would picture them, simply pure light and energy. Another realm took the form of a beautiful garden, which Hermod said he had created simply by visualising it. In that realm of illusion, he explained, people created their own world according to their expectations and conditioning. If they felt guilt they would create their own hell and if they had believed in a heavenly paradise they would experience that too. This was a world beyond time and space, a world of being where you communicated by thought alone and could travel to any location on earth at will or be with anyone you wished merely by expressing that desire. Those who could not accept their own death remained near their bodies and were earthbound ghosts.

On another occasion Elleke met Hermod's mother who had passed over many years before and she learnt that spirits often leave this world to communicate with their loved ones who are still incarnate, but that many of the living are not open or receptive and so they sense the loss and separation more keenly.

Beyond the realm of illusion where desires could assume a transitory form there was a higher state of being. In this elevated dimension of thought mutual creativity prevailed as opposed to individual wish-fulfilment. And beyond this second tier was another, a realm of pure consciousness, a state of being beyond human comprehension where there was no need even for communication or assuming a shape. Here she passed into the 'layer of souls' of pure essence to which we ascend when we have learnt to transcend our sense of self and discard our earthly personality. It was a realm of 'deep love' more real than life on earth.

'At some point', she recalls, 'it became so subtle that my being couldn't stand it.' She had no thoughts, or feelings, or even any sense of her fiancé. She was immersed in light and unconditional love. 'If I could call anything God, and I grew up an atheist, then that would be it. Oneness but consciousness.' Elleke admits that she could only comprehend a fraction of whatever she had connected with because it was too vast to understand and language is too limited to convey its nature or magnitude. She sensed that there were worlds beyond worlds, but she knew she could go no further now.

Elleke believes that her ability to leave her body so effortlessly was due to the trauma she had suffered which had disrupted her connection to the physical world. As the weeks went on she became aware that her desire to be with Hermod and to be free of the pains of separation were having an adverse affect on her ability to look after her children. She appears to have come to the conclusion that the reason why we do not normally have access to the heavenly realms is because if we did experience the rarified atmosphere of the upper worlds we would be reluctant to return and fulfil our responsibilities on earth. At the same time, she became aware that Hermod was becoming less corporeal and more like the beings of pure energy that she had sensed earlier. The marks of his injuries were fading and he looked younger. At first she put this down to the fact that she unconsciously wanted to see him in an idealised form and might be in denial to avoid the pain of bereavement, but she remarks that she had loved him as he was and had no desire to change him. Hermod's presence is still with her, but he comes less often since she made a conscious effort to ground herself in the here and now for the sake of her children. But her out-of-body experiences changed her life forever. 'I am learning to love this life again,' she concludes, 'to live life to the full ... to honour life itself.'

# 7

# Talking to Heaven

I f we want to know what heaven is like, there is only one way to find out short of going there in person and that is by talking to the dead. The most reliable and practical way of doing this for most of us is to consult a medium. In the course of writing this book I have interviewed several psychics whom I have personally found to be uncannily accurate and uncommonly consistent and who were willing to share their insights and experiences in print.

## The psychic cleric

Contrary to popular belief, psychic sensitivity is not limited to New Age eccentrics or middle-aged matronly mediums. Even those who have been conditioned by their cultural and religious upbringing to discount survival evidence as the product of their overactive imagination can experience supernatural phenomena as startling as any demonstrated on the spiritualist stage. Catholic sacristan Tina Hamilton presides over funerals at St Thomas Church, Canterbury, Kent and often senses the presence of the deceased who bring with them a powerfully pervasive sense of peace. As she explains:

> I don't see them. I don't need to. But I hear them and
> feel the force of their personality which evidently
> survives the death of the physical body. Sometimes I
> may even feel them put their arm around my shoulder.
> If it is a particularly strong presence I will strike up a
> telepathic conversation. It's definitely not my
> imagination nor my thoughts. It's their voice that I hear
> loud and clear inside my head. They feel more alive
> than ever and are amazed that their family and friends
> can't see them. They will frequently express surprise and
> satisfaction at the amount of people attending their
> funeral and the degree of love that they generated

*during their lifetime. Some might even laugh at seeing a particular relative who they knew didn't like them, but have turned up begrudgingly out of a sense of duty. If I think about it, it's usually their sense of humour that strikes me most forcibly. Perhaps it's the relief of having left their fears and worldly concerns behind. After the service I am often compelled to ask the family the names of the people that the deceased singled out and it is always just as I was told by the spirit.*

*Never in my 50 years of service to the church have I sensed a spirit in any kind of distress. Although, once I was conducting the funeral service for a teenage girl who had committed suicide, when she came through to express how sorry she was for leaving her parents with all this pain and guilt. She told me that she had suffered psychological problems and depression which I hadn't been told but which her family later confirmed to have been the case.*

*I have encountered unsettled spirits but never in the church. Occasionally I have been in the town minding my own business when I will hear someone call my name and when I turn round there is no one there. Then I will hear it again and that's when I'll realise that it is a spirit. So I'll ask who it is and what they want with me. I need them to identify themselves so I can address them in person as it helps me to connect and establish an empathy with them, but also so that I can later do some research and find out who it was that I was helping. Invariably it's a lost soul who has just died suddenly, unprepared for their passing, and is confused. They want to know what to do next. So I tell them to stay calm and go into the light and moments later I will sense the presence fade as a feeling of peace or relief overwhelms me. I once sensed a presence of a young man who identified himself by name and told me that he had been travelling down from Glasgow when he was involved in a head-on collision on the Thanet Way. He was confused at finding himself wandering around the streets of Canterbury having forgotten how the journey had ended. He kept reliving the accident as if it was a dream that didn't make sense. But even he wasn't distressed, simply confused. My experience leads me to believe that the soul does not suffer even a violent death, but is simply separated from the physical body by the event.*

Tina's psychic experiences began as a child and so feel completely natural to her.

*I remember at the age of five describing the dead people I had seen and my sister tried to frighten me by saying that if I didn't admit I was making it all up men in white coats would come and take me away.*

*I apparently inherited my gift from my maternal grandmother, but my mother encouraged me even though she was a devoutly religious woman. She always said that if you have a talent you must develop it, just like any other ability, or it is an insult to God who gave it to you. Besides, you can't suppress psychic sensitivity for long otherwise it can make you physically and psychologically ill. But you must learn how to 'open up' and 'close down' properly otherwise you risk being overwhelmed by discarnate spirits and mischievous spirits who are drawn to a medium like moths to a flame. In the vast darkness of space you are a lighthouse for any entity, benign or otherwise, who is trying to communicate or re-enter this world.*

*That's why I decided to train as a healer at the SAGB (Spiritualist Association of Great Britain) at their school in London when I was in my twenties. When the course was finished they asked me to stay and become a platform medium but I didn't feel right about doing that. I didn't see any value in passing on mundane messages from Aunty Mabel or Uncle Jim. I wanted to be a healer and bring comfort to the dying. Even if you have a gift I still believe you have a choice as to what to do with it, to decide what use you will put it to.*

*But I was impressed by the mediums at the SAGB. One in particular told me why I had a fear of deep water even though I could swim. She told me that I had drowned in a previous life as a nurse in the Crimea and she quoted places and dates which I was later able to research and found to be true. As soon as she described the incident which ended that lifetime, I knew intuitively, deep down at the core of my being, that she was right. It gave me great relief to know why I had this irrational fear which had hampered me since childhood as all my family were enthusiastic swimmers.*

*My father was Jewish and did not believe in life after death but days after his passing his image appeared simultaneously in each of my sister's homes. Crazy though it might sound they both swore that he had appeared on their TV screens during* Match of the Day, *which was his favourite programme. That proved to me that the personality survives death. As my father used to say, 'you don't grow a halo just because you're dead'. Since then he comes through whenever I am in the presence of a good medium, even though he didn't believe in such things in his lifetime. And what impresses me is that he will give her a message for me in Yiddish which I understand but which the medium has never heard. They will frequently express surprise at receiving what they believe is a garbled message until I reassure them that it is a dialect that I understand.*

*Curiously, my mother did believe in life after death, but she never came through.*

So how does Tina reconcile her religious faith with the idea that religious observance appears to be irrelevant in the spirit world?

*Religion serves as a guide and a great comfort to people during their lifetime and may ease their passing. Once on the other side you still hold the same values.*

And how do her clerical colleagues react to her psychic experiences?

*They will stop me short by saying, 'Now Tina, we don't want to know about that.' Then a while later they'll come round and casually ask, 'so what happened next?'*

# Tamara – all is energy

The Yugoslav healer Tamara Mount recalls the first time that she became conscious of another reality.

*My husband and I were on holiday in Australia in the late 1990s when he fell ill and had to be hospitalised. Shortly before I was due to visit him I decided to lie down on the bed in our hotel room and have five minutes' meditation to prepare myself so that I could deal with the doctors and all the stress of the situation. As it turned out that was the most important five minutes of my life.*

*As I went deeper into relaxation I could feel myself becoming heavier until my body felt like lead. I was rigid, paralysed. I couldn't move. The next moment I was weightless and enfolded in a lovely soft velvety warmth. There was an accompanying scent of sweet walnut which I have sensed on subsequent occasions when I attained this state of what I can only describe as bliss. But words are really inadequate to describe this sensation of detachment from the physical world. Then I felt my mind shooting out of my forehead and ascending at incredible speed high up into the atmosphere toward a whirlwind or a vortex. When I looked back on the earth far below everything was dark around me, not a blackness but a deep indigo blue.*

*I was floating in that space tethered to my body by what looked like a long elasticated rope.*

*I was aware of being both out of my body and also in my body at the same time. I was acutely aware of being in two dimensions at the same time, but I wasn't afraid. It was bliss and it felt completely natural at the time.*

*When I finally drifted back into my body I looked at the clock and discovered that I had been out for 45 minutes, but during that experience I existed in a state beyond time and space.*

*I was exhilarated and wanted to know what it meant and how I could make it happen again. I became addicted to that sense of bliss. And that fuelled my desire to learn everything I could about our true nature and the nature of the universe.*

*Being a very analytical person I wanted to understand what it was that I was experiencing and not simply dismiss it as a phenomenon. So, I chose to investigate step by step to see how I could consciously achieve that state at will instead of involuntarily. I practised meditation on a regular basis and explored the subtle energies that I sensed around me through spiritual healing. I began to see the colours of the human aura, both around myself and emanating from the patients I was treating. One time had a flash of insight when I looked at my husband and saw that he had two broken ribs. It was like an x-ray. He had taken a fall while playing rugby and thought he just had a bruise, but I persuaded him to see a doctor and I was proven right. Another time he was complaining about a swollen foot, for which he used to take anti-inflammatory drugs to reduce the swelling, and it would take a week to go down. On this occasion I could 'see' that the pain was caused by a build-up of crystals in the muscle so I gave him healing three times that day and by the next day the swelling had gone completely. We can all do this for each other, but there are vested interests in maintaining a drug-dependent society. The pharmaceutical companies would go bust, for example, and so there is a culture of discrediting healers and denying the existence of our latent psychic abilities.*

*The thrill I got from healing people became quite addictive. I would deliberately create a vortex of energy by visualising it so that I could raise my awareness to other levels which gave me both some of the most enlightening, but also some of the most frightening experiences I have had. I remember once coming face to face with this demon-like being. I knew that if I gave in to my fear I wouldn't have the courage to explore this any more so I confronted it, told it that I loved it and it turned into a petal.*

It sounds as if it was a personification of your own anxieties, an inner demon embodying your fear of the unknown or of what you might find if you continued to explore?

*Yes, I'm sure it was because I always began a meditation by asking to be taken to wherever I need to go and to experience whatever I need to experience. So that fiery 'demon' would have been a predictable response. At some point in this journey of self-discovery you have to face your own fears and many people don't evolve and mature spiritually because they are not prepared to do that. But when you are, you will discover that there is nothing to fear but fear itself, to borrow a tired but true cliché. I don't personally believe in evil as a conscious entity and despite what I have just described, I have never encountered malevolent beings. It's all energy. We are energy confined in matter, everything in the universe is energy and energy is neutral. It depends how you use it. The principle of the universe is energy–thought–matter so whatever you visualise, you create on a mental, psychological and physical level. We create a temporary reality in our dreams, but we can also create a fantasy in the 'real' world with our thoughts, wishes, fears and daydreams and if we empower them with emotional energy we give them a reality which, if negative, can make us mentally or physically ill. Many illnesses are psychosomatic in origin and that is why I never treat the symptoms but go straight to the source. Passive healers lay their hands on a patient and can alleviate a lot of suffering, but it invariably returns because they haven't addressed the cause. Every cell in our bodies is a living aspect of our being and is affected by the state of our psyche. So we can make ourselves literally sick with worry, or effect a miraculous cure depending upon our state of mind.*

*We have the ability to process the universal life force through what I choose to call receptors in our brain, which channels the regenerative force through our thoughts into matter. This is how active imagination (visualisation) exercises and positive thinking works. Our brains are like a supercomputer with six major decoders – senses, hearing, seeing, self and communication. Every cell can be likened to a file with the equivalent of indexes located in our joints. In this way the body has a memory which can be conditioned by experience to trigger instinctive reactions or reflexes.*

90

This would explain why and how we invented the technology we now possess. Computers, communication systems and even medical treatments are not a miraculous advance invented in a flash of inspiration but an expression or extension of our own psychic cognitive processes and capacity.

> *Yes. But the more we progress technically the weaker our primitive psychic sensitivities become which our ancestors possessed in order to sense danger or to divine water, for example. As the population has grown we have become disconnected from each and so need an artificial extension (the telephone) in order to communicate. And similarly, as we developed medicines and sophisticated surgical treatments we lost the need and ability to heal each other. Those who can communicate on a subtle (i.e. psychic) level and heal with just the heat from their hands are in the minority and considered as freaks. This is the true price of progress.*

As Tamara's sensitivity increased, she sensed the energies that surround and emanate from us more acutely. A sick person would have a muddy aura around the affected area, making it look as if it had been polluted, which is effectively what happens when a virus infects us or there is dis-ease in the psyche.

During healing she has also experienced a heightened awareness of other realities and been aided by those beings we might choose to call angels.

> *I remember treating a woman who had come to me for healing, but as always I didn't want to know what her symptoms were. I wanted to be guided to the source without being told. So I asked her to lie on a couch and then I ran my hands over her sensing for a cold spot which could indicate where the trouble originated. Moments later I was drawn to her stomach and when she saw that I was concentrating on that spot she told me that she had suffered chronic stomach and back pains for many years. It was then that I smelt the scent of lavender, which told me that a presence was near. But it was a distinctly old-fashioned fragrance more like a disinfectant than a perfume. Although my eyes were open I saw a second scene superimposed over the room we were working in. It was a nineteenth-century*

91

*amphitheatre like the kind where medical students came to watch a surgical operation with an operating table in the centre. As I was looking at this I could feel my body stiffen, just like it had done when I had the out-of-body experience. I couldn't move. I couldn't even speak. I was locked up. Then a huge figure robed in blue appeared and asked me if I wanted to see a miracle. I felt I was in the presence of God, or an aspect of God. Whatever you want to call it, it was overwhelming and I had to summon all my will not to pass out. He put his hand on my patient's stomach and pulled something out which looked like a piece of meat and said simply, 'that's it'. At that instant my patient gasped, 'have I given birth or something?'*

*She had felt something being pulled from her stomach and assumed that I had done something physical to her, but I hadn't. As the robed figure left and the vision faded I went weak at the knees and thought I would faint. Since then the lady hasn't suffered any more pain in her stomach or back.*

Tamara's experiences of the various levels and qualities of energy have led her to form a radical new theory of the nature of the universe and the life cycle of the soul.

*Whenever I tapped into a new source of energy through meditation, or as the result of a specific spiritual experience, I would see the colour and feel the quality associated with that level. So now I can't accept the traditional concept of a single heavenly paradise to which we all return after death. I see the universe like a sort of family tree with a series of lesser dimensions emanating from the source, or God, if you prefer. Those individuals who are more self-aware and developed will have originated from the highest of these worlds and those of lesser ability and awareness from the worlds closer to our earthly plane, where the influence of the source has been diluted to a greater degree. So instead of there being one tunnel of light leading to a heavenly paradise for all souls, it is my belief that each soul returns to its home dimension. However, if someone evolves sufficiently through their experiences on earth they may ascend to a higher level and so evolve with*

*each successive lifetime until they can reunite with the
source.*

## Jill Nash – a wealth of experience

Since childhood, Kent psychic medium Jill Nash had been convinced that
our physical world is only one aspect of a greater reality but it was not until
she was 16 years old that a near-death experience confirmed what she had
intuitively known.

*When I was 16 I was hospitalised with viral
pneumonia, a very serious illness. The doctors doubted
that I would pull through so they sent for my mother
and father and told them that I was at a critical point in
the illness.*

*After they'd gone I remember lying in bed and seeing
something curious at the end of my bed. It was a
beautiful, bright, pulsating, strong white light. I
couldn't see anything in the light but I had the strongest
sense that there was a presence in the middle of it which
was communicating with me. In my mind I could hear
it say, 'We are not ready for you yet. You still have a lot
to do in this life.' That was the first time I had
confirmation that there is a next step after this life, here
on earth. I wasn't afraid at all. I was calm, relaxed and
peaceful. It was a reassuring presence and I wanted to
go to it because I had been very ill and I knew that by
entering the light the sickness and anxiety would be
taken away. I can't describe what was in the light but I
felt it was an all-embracing energy, a lot of
unconditional love and understanding.*

*I must have drifted off to sleep then because the next
thing I knew I was awake, the fever had gone and I was
inclined to dismiss the experience as a dream or
something I had imagined brought on by the illness or
medication. And in a sense it was imagination because
we can only perceive another reality and higher
frequencies or vibrations of energy through our sixth
and more acute sense which we call our imagination.*

*Unfortunately I couldn't tell my parents because they
were strict Methodists and sneered at any form of*

*psychic phenomenon. Frankly, I think they were frightened of anything which challenged their faith. It made them uncomfortable. I used to sense a presence occasionally and my mother would shut me up by shouting, 'I don't want to hear about dead people.' But I was never scared because I know nothing really dies. Energy can't die. It can only be transformed.*

That experience led directly to Jill's lifelong commitment to helping the bereaved attain some measure of comfort and closure by facilitating a reunion with their loved ones.

*On one particularly memorable occasion I opened the door expecting to see a little elderly lady and instead saw her and her late husband. He walked in behind her. She was, of course, unaware that he was with her but I could see him plain as day, although he was fainter than a living person, almost transparent and there was nothing to see below the knee. He was tall and slim and when she sat down he stood behind her with a satisfied grin on his face as if he was thinking, 'at last, now I can tell her what I have been trying to say to her for months'.*

*As soon as we were settled he communicated to me telepathically, mind to mind, that he wanted me to tell her about a rose. Of course I didn't know what he meant, I hadn't met this lady before. But she did. He had apparently been trying to create a new type of rose by grafting and it hadn't taken while he was alive but he wanted her to keep the plant alive because he knew it was going to work. I described the plant and the type of pot it was in and the fact that it was underneath the front window of their bungalow. Of course I had never seen their house but I could see it in my mind as he transferred his thoughts to mine.*

*He wanted her to know that he was all right and that he was with her if she wanted to say anything or share her feelings. He told me to tell her that he often stood behind her when she sat in her armchair in the evenings and that if she felt something like a cobweb brushing against her cheek or a gentle pat on the head that it was only him reassuring her that he was still around. And as soon as I said that, she admitted that she had felt these things and had wondered if it was him, although she couldn't trust her own feelings or believe that he was really there.*

They say that for those who believe in life after death, no proof is necessary and for those who do not believe, no proof is enough. But, as Jill discovered, some people need proof twice over before they are finally convinced.

*I was offering past-life readings at a psychic fayre when I was approached by a man who made a great show of being a cynic. He was obviously proud of his scepticism and approached me as a form of challenge. In fact he said, 'if you can tell me exactly what I was told a few weeks ago by someone else then I might believe in life after death'. I wasn't going to be bullied so I silently asked for help from my friends up there, my guides in spirit, and I immediately felt as if I was being flown backwards on a flying carpet. That's the sensation I have when I connect with someone's past life. I saw this man as he had been in an earlier century. He was a Turkish merchant haggling in a bazaar. He looked different to the way he does in this life but it was him. It was the same personality in a different body. When I described what I was seeing he was absolutely gobsmacked and staggered out as if he had been bopped between the eyes.*

*Another time I gave a reading to an elderly man who I sensed carried a great burden with him from life to life. As I held his hands to make the connection I saw in my mind a scene of him and a woman as they had been in an earlier incarnation and then again as they are now. I told him that there was a recurring, unresolved conflict between the two of them and that the source of this problem was a disagreement over property, just as it had been in a previous life. She had followed him through from life to life because she had felt cheated and wanted him to make amends.*

*When I had finished the reading he told me that I had just described his ex-wife and that their relationship had been dominated by a disagreement over their property and that he had always suspected that her resentment and distrust were so strong that it must have originated in a past life because the present quarrel hadn't merited such strong feelings. So that shows what can happen when you can't let go of something or somebody. You bind yourself to them and by doing so hold back your own progress.*

Perhaps the most revealing insight a person can have into the nature of life, death and rebirth is what is known as a past-life recollection. This unconscious memory of a previous existence can be recalled spontaneously and involuntarily, or at will through a technique known as past-life regression. Jill re-experienced an incident from a past life with full sensory awareness which was subsequently corroborated.

*Several years ago I went to what is known in psychic circles as a 'fledgling evening', which is the name given to a meeting of people who wish to develop their psychic gifts under the guidance of an experienced teacher. On this occasion the group was being led by a highly regarded Jungian psychologist and qualified counsellor called Nanette Philips.*

*I didn't know Ms Philips at that time, but I had a nagging suspicion that I had seen her somewhere before as soon as I entered the room. In fact, the feeling became so strong I had to ask if we had met before. She said we hadn't but then asked me to close my eyes, relax and describe what I felt or saw. I felt a bit awkward doing that with everyone looking at me, but I did as she asked and was soon overcome by a tingling and terrific heat all over my body. That was strange because we were in a chilly hall in the middle of winter. The heat became so intense that I began to sweat. It was then that I saw images of Ancient Egypt and saw myself in a vast temple. Ms Philips was there too, but not as she is now. She was dressed as a priestess of Isis and was cowering behind me as a large, imposing man approached. I lost all sense of where I was physically and was literally transported back in time.*

*I described aloud to the group what I was seeing and as soon as I mentioned the man I heard Ms Philips take a sharp intake of breath. He was stern and very, very*

*threatening. He was covered from head to foot in red
ochre body paint and wore a short pleated skirt-type
dress and a gold armband embossed with a cobra. A
thick scar ran from his right wrist to his elbow and part
of his left ear was missing. It seemed to me as though he
had come to take her to be killed for something she had
done or been accused of doing. She was to be put to
death by the bite of a poisonous snake – the thought of
which gave me a shiver as I have always had an
irrational fear of snakes and this might explain why.
The man wasn't after me, but I was still terrified. It
became so bad that I had to come out of it, shaken and
exhausted.*

*It was then that Ms Philips revealed that she had
recently been to a regression therapist and everything I
had described she herself had seen during that session.
Moreover, the session had been recorded and she
promised to bring the tape in the next day for our
second meeting so that we could all hear that what I
had seen and experienced had been shared by the two
of us. But that wasn't the end of it. The following day I
went to the local library to see if I could find any books
about Ancient Egypt to shed some light on what I had
seen and on the inner flap of the dust jacket of the first
book I picked up there was a photo of the very same
gold armband that I had seen, complete with the
serpent symbol. It was identical.*

In spite of, or perhaps because of, that experience Egypt still held a
fascination for Jill, in fact her interest in the country and its history
intensified. So in 1996 she went there on holiday.

*As the tour guide was explaining their customs and
culture I turned to my husband and said quietly, 'it was
different in ancient times', and described what I
intuitively knew to be the way they lived. A moment
later the guide said, 'of course in the days of the
pharaohs they did X, Y and Z' and repeated the details
of the scene I had just described.*

*The same happened when we visited the ruins of the
temple of Isis at Karnak. As the guide was describing
the way the interior looked at the time of the pharaohs,*

*I turned to my husband and described the scene in detail, with the hanging silk drapes and other details which the guide didn't comment upon until later.*

*But the longer we stayed at the site the more oppressive the atmosphere became until I was overcome and suffered an epileptic fit. I had obviously felt the need to return to that place to find some sort of closure, as the bereavement counsellors call it, but it just brought back the emotional distress. I'm now convinced that I had been a handmaiden and was killed for defending my mistress by the man with the cobra armband. The method of murder for women at that time was death from the bite of a poisonous snake and that, I am absolutely certain, accounts for my fear of snakes.*

*One of the most profound experiences I had was the day my older sister Pat died. She had pancreatic cancer and had been given just a few days to live. I was desperate to be there at the end and prayed to be given a week with her, which is exactly what we had together.*

*On the last day they brought her bed downstairs and I sat with her together with a nurse who was there to make my sister as comfortable as possible. I pulled my chair right up close to the bed so that she could hear me and held her hand. I told her that there was nothing to be afraid of, that she had done this so many times before as we all have. I told her that she would be met on the other side by those who loved her, maybe even by my beautiful dog Beau, a golden retriever, who had died just a few months before. I told her I would take her as far as I could and then began to describe the tunnel of light which I could see in my mind's eye but also sense as a radiant energy all around us. I talked her through the journey to the other side and as I did so I could hear from her breathing that she was following me.*

*This must have gone on for some considerable time, but I was out of it, I had no sense of time or the physical world I had left behind. Then just as the dawn came up she passed away. I heard the rattle of her last breath and knew she was gone. She went very peacefully. I opened my eyes and the nurse said that was the most beautiful thing she had ever heard and wished I could be at the hospice where she worked to guide all the terminally ill patients through the process of dying. So many of them would love that, she told me.*

*A few weeks later I went to a psychic evening at a local spiritualist church and a trainee medium who I'd never met approached me and told me that she had a message for me. She described the lady who was coming through to her which was an exact image of Pat. Then she said that my sister had a gorgeous dog with her, a golden retriever, which was the confirmation I needed that Pat had passed safely to the other side. The medium told me that Pat wanted to say 'thank you' for helping her across and to tell me that I had been right about what I said would happen and what it was like on the other side.*

If that wasn't sufficient confirmation of survival after death then Jill certainly received all she needed a few years later.

*My younger sister was later diagnosed with terminal lung cancer and again I asked the angels and my friends in spirit for a week's grace so that I could be with her at the end and again my prayers were answered. I had exactly a week with her before she passed away. On the last day I propped her up in her chair and we were talking quietly when she began fighting for breath and when the coughing fit had passed she turned to me and said, 'Let me go, I can't go on like this.' So I asked for her to go peacefully and without having to endure any further suffering. The doctor had assured me she might last another few days, or a week at most, but a few hours later she suddenly sat up and opened her eyes. It was totally unexpected because she had been heavily sedated and appeared to have no strength left in her. But she was wide awake and she seemed to be fixed on a point near the ceiling as if she could see something there that I couldn't. Then she said with pleasing surprise, 'Oh, Pat. Pat is here', referring to my older sister who had died a few years earlier. She asked me if I could see Pat but I couldn't, although I did sense a wave of calm come over me. There was definitely a presence in that corner of the room. And then with a smile she was gone. When the doctor came to give the death certificate he couldn't believe that she had gone so quickly, but I wasn't surprised. I had asked that spirit should end her suffering and they did.*

Jill's experience seems to be typical of what are commonly known as 'deathbed visions', in which dying patients unaccountably become momentarily lucid and describe seeing a bright white light from where their deceased relatives appear to beckon them to join them in the world beyond. Such visions are often witnessed by nurses and carers who may have been sceptical about life after death themselves, but who are impressed by the dramatic change in the patient and the return of their former personality before the delirium returns or death occurs.

It would seem that when we die we remain the same personalities we were in life, but we discard our fears and concerns that made us earthbound and materialistic.

Jill remembers with fondness a small incident which demonstrated that her father had not lost his mischievous sense of humour when he passed over.

*I went to an open day at Stansted College, which is popularly known as England's 'psychic school'. Some of the best mediums in the country were giving readings in various rooms and my friends and I began our 'tour' in the main hall which was filled to capacity with several hundred people. We were standing at the back when the medium said that he had to interrupt his demonstration because he was being literally nagged by a spirit who was insisting he be allowed to come through. It was an elderly man by the name of Percy who had passed over 20 years ago. The medium described Percy and his habits including his compulsive need to pat his hair and the fact that one of his fingers was missing. And it was my dad! He had lost a finger in a factory accident when he was a young man. He just wanted to tell me that he was fine and that I had been right about what I told him would be waiting for him on the other side.*

*But the funniest thing was that when I went on to watch a demonstration of direct voice mediumship in the next room my dad's spirit followed me and said 'hello' again through that medium. The medium actually spoke in his voice which I recognised immediately. And if that wasn't enough he did it again*

> *in the next room through another medium, so then I*
> *had to tell him to stop and give someone else a turn!*

It is not uncommon for young children to recall incidents from a past life, or even the moment of their death because they are still receptive to impressions from the unconscious or higher self and have not yet learnt to fear the unknown. They haven't been conditioned to rationalise their experiences and dismiss them as mere imagination. For the same reason they are more likely to see apparitions and take such encounters in their stride, particularly if they are family members who have passed on. It is not until about the age of five that children lose that connection with the other world and become firmly grounded in physical reality.

Jill recalls a small but significant incident with her then three-year-old grandson Jason which is fairly typical for children of this age.

> *Jason lay flat on the floor and told me casually that this*
> *is how he had died. I must have looked shocked*
> *because he reassured me that it wasn't bad as he had*
> *been very old and he had had lots of children. That*
> *rang true because he has always liked looking after*
> *younger children. Then he said something very curious.*
> *He said after he had died he went through 'the gate'. I*
> *hadn't heard such an expression before, but he didn't*
> *want to talk about it any more except to reassure me*
> *that he was fine after that and that he had now come*
> *back. It was only months later that I read that going*
> *'through the gate' was a common expression among a*
> *particular Christian sect in the north of England during*
> *the nineteenth century.*
>
> *Later that day I was flicking through a family photo*
> *album when Jason looked over my shoulder, pointed to*
> *my father in a crowded group and told me that this was*
> *the man who used to play with him, but that he didn't*
> *come very often any more. When I mentioned this to my*
> *daughter she told me that she had often heard him*
> *talking and laughing while he was playing and had*
> *asked him who he was talking to. And he had said, 'Oh,*
> *its only grandad'. That was astounding because his*
> *grandfather had died before Jason was born.*

# Viviane – talking to the dead

As with many mediums, London psychic Viviane Harbourne had been a lonely child, considered an outsider by her classmates because she appeared to live in a world of her own. But the world she played in wasn't created by her imagination.

> To me, seeing dead people was natural. I didn't even realise that they were dead because they appeared alive to me. It was only later when I thought about the old-fashioned way that they were dressed that I realised that they were apparitions. But they were alive in the sense that they were real personalities and that is why I wasn't frightened. Ghosts are real people who have simply left their body just as we would discard an overcoat. They don't go around clanking chains and making weird noises. They are not scary unless you believe that they are unnatural. If you don't believe in life after death, then I imagine their appearance would be very unsettling. But they look like you and me. They would be there to warn me that there were other kids nearby who were looking to beat me up, or to tell me that I shouldn't be playing in a certain place which might be where they had died. I remember being told off severely about something by an old lady dressed in black in the ladies lavatory in a cinema and all I could think was 'why is she dressed in Victorian clothes?'. Being a child I just accepted that there were adults who appeared wherever you shouldn't be to keep children out of trouble.

Viviane admits that the other reason she was unpopular was that she was considered to be 'a little prophet of doom'.

> They didn't like me being around them because I could sense if something bad was going to happen and would try to warn them, which of course only unnerved them. There was one boy in particular who would be constantly told by his friends and teachers that he was going to be successful, but I felt that he wouldn't live much longer. I actually saw right through him as if he wasn't here. Sometimes I would feel compelled to hang around a zebra crossing where I knew this boy would have an accident and one day that's where he was run

*over and killed. After that, I learnt not to tell others
what I sensed about them.*

Even out-of-body experiences were accepted with the artless innocence
of a child.

> *My first OBE occurred when I was nine years old after I
> had been in hospital for some weeks with a viral
> infection. I remember having a nosebleed and using up
> all the tissues by my bed to clean up the blood which
> was dripping onto the sheets. I got in quite a panic
> worrying that I would be told off for messing up the bed
> when suddenly it started spinning and rising up into the
> air. It must have been a dream triggered by my
> unconscious to accompany the sensation of floating free
> of my body. The next moment I sank into black
> nothingness and the bed was back on the ground. I
> started to climb out of the bed and as I did so I
> discovered that I wasn't solid any more and floated free
> of my body all the way up to the ceiling. But something
> prevented me from going any further. I could look down
> on myself lying in the bed. From there I saw a man who
> I took to be a priest walk along the glass-panelled
> corridor into my room. He sat down by my bed and
> began to read me a story. I remember it was 'Joseph and
> the Coat of Many Colours' and I desperately wanted to
> hear it. So I pulled myself back down to earth by
> yanking on this cord that connected me to my body and
> climbed back in. When I opened my eyes the priest had
> gone and the nurses were fussing around me cleaning
> up the blood. I still don't know if he was real or a being
> who had been sent to draw me back down to earth, but
> the sensation of being free of my physical body was
> exhilarating and reassuringly peaceful at the same time.
> It remains as vivid and as real to me today when I recall
> it as it was nearly forty years ago.*

When Viviane opens herself up to possession by spirits she gets a
sense of the dimension from which they have come.

> *I don't see heaven as such, but I do get a strong sense
> of a place which I can only describe as home. There is a
> profound sense of security and peace, but then as they
> take form and their previous personality asserts itself I*

*only sense the environment they knew the last time they
were alive on earth. When they leave I have a sense
that they have returned to the peaceful oblivion of
darkness. I cannot see beyond that.*

One would hope that having made the effort to materialise they would
offer some profound insight into the nature of existence or bring a sense of
purpose to those they have left behind, but frequently their message is
mundane or even trivial and they speak in such bland generalities. It
suggests that they may not be messengers from heaven but earthbound
spirits from a transitory stage in which they rest between lives. It is
significant that the spirits who communicate through mediums are
frequently only one generation removed from the person they wish to speak
to. Presumably grandparents and ancestors have either ascended to the
next level or been reborn and are therefore not available for consultation.

*I think we only receive comparatively mundane
messages because we are not able to understand
anything beyond that. At our stage of development it
would be like giving Einstein's theory of relativity to a
toddler.*

*When I go into a trance I feel removed from what we
call reality, from this physical world. Its like I have
shifted to another level of awareness. Afterwards I have
only a vague recollection of what has been said.
Occasionally, I may re-experience their death, but
unless it's a particularly peaceful passing I will sense
their reluctance to face it and I'll ask my guides to take
that memory away to relieve them of it. I often come out
of a trance to find that I've been crying, but it was not
my feelings that will have triggered it. They use me as a
vessel to clear themselves of residual emotions.*

*Often if a spirit wants to communicate through me I will
sense its presence following me around for hours, or
even days before I meet the person that they want to
contact. I might also smell a fragrance associated with
that person during their lifetime, a favourite perfume for
a woman or maybe a smell of tobacco with a man who
smoked. That scent also helps to identify them so that
the living contact has confirmation so they are receptive
to the rest of the message. When I let the spirit take over
it's my voice you hear, so you won't get their accent, but*

*you will be able to recognise their mannerisms and way of speaking.*

*They always come with one of my guides and a presence I call a gatekeeper, who stand on either side of me. I can differentiate between the two spirit guides and the deceased by the quality of their energy. I first became aware of these two protecting presences the first time I was being 'nagged' by a spirit who wanted to take me over. I told it that I wasn't supposed to do this on my own and I heard a voice reply that I wasn't on my own.*

*Once I have opened myself to be used in this way I can't choose to end it. Even if the spirit is disturbed I have to let the session come to a natural conclusion and allow it to leave of its own accord. I can't cast it out. But even the more disturbed personalities don't affect me. If they haven't dealt with whatever disturbs them and taken the opportunity to clear it, then they have to take it with them. I am not left with a sense of their presence once they've departed. I have never felt in any danger. They're just people. Whether dead or alive you're only dealing with people. And if they make you uncomfortable then you just have to be firm with them and tell them that you're closing off to them today and ask them to come back another time.*

There is compelling experiential evidence that we can expand our consciousness not only to other locations but also to other levels of awareness, perhaps even to glimpse the future. Such phenomena may seem illogical and unscientific, but if we accept that our minds are a form of mental energy not confined to the brain then it is possible that we can survey the world ahead just as easily as we can recall the past.

*Some years ago my guides told me that my life was about to change dramatically and that I would meet the man who would become my teacher. They told me that he would be a builder by profession and then they gave me a glimpse of the future. It was a vision of a hotel room, which didn't mean anything to me at the time. But a short while later I met Mike who was a builder and who became my spiritual teacher, just as I had been told. Later we were married and went to Torquay for our honeymoon. The moment we entered our hotel room I recognised it as being the scene from my vision. I'd never been to Torquay, so there was no way that I could have recalled this place from an earlier visit.*

Viviane's husband, Michael, is also a trance medium and freely admits he does not conform to the typical image of a practising psychic who converses routinely with the spirits of the dear departed. A builder by trade he remains a devout sceptic despite having led psychic development circles for the past 14 years, during which he has received compelling evidence of life after death.

*I have always prided myself on being down to earth, but I see my scepticism as healthy. It prompts me to question and seek confirmation for everything I receive from spirit.*

Michael answered his calling comparatively late in life at the age of 42 after being shaken to the core by two 'emotional shocks' which left him so depressed that he sought healing at his local spiritualist church, albeit against his better judgement.

*Afterwards there was a demonstration of clairvoyance in the church hall next door and I went out of sheer curiosity. The medium gave me convincing evidence that my late father was with me and then astonished me by announcing that I would be doing what he was doing within seven years. I dismissed it as a theatrical gesture, but he has been proven right. Over the course of the next few weeks I began attending a circle three times a week. At first I saw colours, then three-dimensional shapes and then pairs of eyes staring back at me as my third-eye centre opened. Finally I began to receive messages in the form of intrusive thoughts which I wrote down so that I would have a record of my experiences.*

*At the end of one meeting I was taken aside by the medium and told that he had seen the spirit of a very famous trance medium sitting next to me and that he had been told that I should have been a doctor, not a builder. That was a real shock because only my close family knew that I had been offered a place at medical school when I was younger and that I had turned it down. Then he said that I was going to travel to the US within three years and that the trip would be significant, not a holiday. Again he was right. Three years later, almost to the day, I was invited to see someone in America, which was important to my life and it wasn't a trip that I could have arranged or foreseen. That told me that there are key stages like stepping stones that we have to arrive at in life but that we can exercise our free will during the bits in between.*

Disembodied spirits are not the only inhabitants of the worlds beyond our own, it seems. On several occasions Mike was told by various mediums that he had a Native American guide who stood behind him, and they each described his guide in exactly the same way. But he remained stubbornly sceptical until one evening when, as if in answer to his doubts, he felt a forceful whack round the back of his head and felt something take possession of him.

*I wasn't afraid as I was no longer me. I was the Native American and was chanting and speaking in his voice. I was fully conscious of having been taken over and kept thinking, 'he's never going to go', but after five minutes or so (though it seemed much longer), I felt another whack around the back of the head and he was gone. Since then I have been a channel for Chinese and other spirit guides.*

*Now my guides come to every meeting of our circle, but I never call them by name because I think that if I did I might be unconsciously creating them in my imagination. So I simply open up and if their face appears spontaneously and the image is sustained of its own volition then I can trust it to be genuine.*

## Hotline to heaven

One of the most respected and best-known spiritual mediums in the world today is the American James Van Praagh, author of the No.1 *New York Times* bestseller *Talking to Heaven* and presenter of the worldwide syndicated US TV show *Beyond*. During the year the show was aired the jovial, diminutive Californian offered astounding survival evidence to his studio guests, who verified virtually everything he told them about their loved ones' lives and the circumstances of their deaths. Occasionally a discarnate spirit would identify the person responsible for their premature passing, which the police would subsequently verify, or reveal a contributing factor which the family had been previously been unaware of – again the new information would be corroborated. Often the details of the death were harrowing, but just as frequently the message would reaffirm the need for the surviving family members to move on and enjoy their lives. But no matter how moving the message he always conveyed it in his non-judgemental manner and with sensitivity and compassion. If anyone can convince a sceptic of the existence of life after death it is James Van Praagh. He discovered his intuitive gifts in childhood when he correctly predicted that one of his teacher's sons would break his leg in a car accident, but survive. Naturally the poor woman didn't receive the warning too graciously, but she was strangely reassured when the prophecy proved accurate. Van Praagh told reporter Alex Witchell of the *New York Times*:

> We're all like radio stations, transmitting and receiving. TV, radios, cellphones all send waves through the air we don't see but we're able to receive a picture, get the sound. It's the same thing. I don't know why it's so hard for people to believe this.

Van Praagh's spiritual guides say he can sense whether he is communicating with an old soul or one that has recently passed on by the quality of their energy. They have told him that there are many levels to heaven and that we gravitate to the level we have created by our thoughts, words and deeds while on earth.

In June 2005 he told *Venture Inward* magazine that the beliefs of a deceased individual can have an impact on their afterlife experience.

> Some people become earthbound, because they have unfinished business here, or they're not aware of their own death, or perhaps they don't even believe in life after death. Other people are very religious and go to a place that corresponds to the Bible's statement: 'In my Father's house are many mansions.' I believe that means you go to the spiritual level that you've evolved to – you're at the same level with people who share your understanding. There are those above you with a greater understanding and those – who are not as aware – below you. On the earth we're all thrown in together. But in the spirit world you go to that level that you've created based on your thoughts, your words, your deeds, and how you treated people. It's almost like you create your own heaven or hell based upon how you lived in this earth. I've also seen it happen where the deceased really hold on to their preconceived notions

*about what death is like, even when they're dead. For example, I've had it happen where people think death means you are unaware, simply waiting around to be raised from the dead. And I tell them, 'You're already dead,' but they insist, 'No, I'm not. I'm still alive.' Otherwise, their experience doesn't match up with their belief system. They're still at that mindset.*

But their predicament is temporary?

*Absolutely. But it's hard enough to change the mind of someone who is living and stubborn or narrow-minded. Imagine what it's like over there. In some ways it's easier to change here than it is over there. The same goes for habits and addictions. It's easier to break habits here than it is over there, because the spirit world is a very mental world. But if people are open to changing their understanding, it can happen … There is really a lot of fear in the world. One of my jobs is to alleviate the fear of death.*

# 8

# Reincarnation and Past-life Regression

*Birth is not a beginning; death is not an end.*

(Chuang Tzu)

US General George S. Patton prided himself on being a plain-speaking, pragmatic man who did not suffer fools gladly. But in December 1917 the 22-year-old military genius arrived in the French town of Langres to take up his post as tank instructor and surprised the local liaison officer by declining his offer of a tour of the town. 'You don't have to,' explained Patton with an enigmatic grin, 'I know it well.' He then proceeded to give his escort a tour of the Roman encampment which he claimed to remember from a former life as a legionnaire. He pointed out the amphitheatre, the temples, the drill ground, the forum and the spot where Julius Caesar had billeted his troops.

Patton's firm belief in reincarnation led him to credit his tactical genius and military success in World War Two to his past-life experiences in various historical campaigns. When complimented on his victories in North Africa by a British general, who observed that he would have made a great marshal in Napoleon's army, Patton casually replied, 'But I did.'

Belief in reincarnation and the transmigration of souls is almost universal and predates all the world religions. Although the idea is fundamental to Eastern philosophy, it is by no means certain that it originated in that region. Many primitive cultures prepared their dead in a manner that attests to their belief in rebirth. For example, several New Stone Age tribes (c.10,000 – 5,000 BC) buried their dead in the foetal position in anticipation of their rebirth.

Several Australian and African tribes share a belief that the soul actively seeks out a parent to whom they wish to be reborn and for this reason they look upon each person they meet as someone they may have known in a previous incarnation. The same is true of certain Native

110

American tribes who bury their children by the side of a road in the hope that the soul will be attracted to a passing female.

The people of Papua New Guinea take this one step further and refrain from killing fish and certain animals in the belief that they may be their ancestors reborn.

The Zulus too share an idea with cultures many thousands of miles away – that of an immortal soul animated by a spark of the divine (i tongo) which reunites with the source once the person has evolved to a point at which it is no longer necessary to reincarnate.

## The curious case of the Cathars

In 533 AD the Christian Church decreed belief in reincarnation to be a heresy, but there were many disaffected Catholics during the Middle Ages who were determined to defy the edict. The most militant of these were the Cathars (meaning 'purified ones') who were persecuted by the ironically titled Pope Innocent III and forced to seek refuge in 1243 behind the walls of their stronghold at Montségur in the French Pyrenees. After a year-long siege the 210 survivors were brought before the Inquisition and tortured in an effort to force them to renounce their beliefs. They all refused and were burnt at the stake.

The fate of the Cathars might have been a footnote in history had it not been for the nightmares of an English housewife more than seven hundred years later. Her testimony remains the single most persuasive argument to date for the existence of the soul group, a family of like-minded souls who reincarnate together so as to help each other evolve through their shared experiences.

In 1962 'Mrs Smith' consulted psychiatrist Arthur Guirdham, complaining of severe headaches and recurrent nightmares. Curiously, Dr Guirdham had for several years suffered from a strikingly similar nightmare, which began with a man entering a room in which he was imprisoned. After their first meeting both doctor and patient ceased to be tormented by these dreams.

Further apparent 'coincidences' aroused the psychiatrist's interest. Both he and Mrs Smith were fascinated and at the same time unsettled by any mention of Montségur, which they had visited independently, at a time when neither of them were aware of the history surrounding the site. Moreover, when she was there, despite never having visited the region previously, Mrs Smith was overcome with the feeling that she *had* been there before and she was able to find her way around the nearby town of St Jean Pied de Port without a map.

Under hypnosis she revealed detailed knowledge of the sect that only specialists could have known. In fact, some of the details she supplied contradicted the official histories, but were later found to be correct. Moreover, it transpired that as a teenager she had written authentic poetry in a dialect of Occitan, the language of southern France in the Middle Ages, that would have tested the scholarship of the most eminent academics.

During the time Dr Guirdham was treating Mrs Smith he came into contact with a further eight individuals who casually professed an interest in the region and subsequently recalled a former life as a Cathar. The curious circumstances under which he met them convinced Dr Guirdham that they were predestined to meet. The first of these was an otherwise pragmatic RAF officer who had once climbed Montségur when unaware of its history and was then overcome with a feeling of extreme nausea and a belief that the site was bathed in blood.

Under Dr Guirdham's supervision the group underwent collective regression sessions which revealed further particulars of their life together at Montségur including obscure domestic details which again contradicted the accepted view of the period, but which were later confirmed. Then on the anniversary of their martyrdom, several members claimed to suffer physical pain and another exhibited blisters as if the skin had been burnt by fire.

Dr Guirdham was not a fanciful man and he was fiercely proud of his reputation and standing in the profession. He was also a methodical person by nature and maintained a healthy scepticism until he could prove or disprove all of the facts to his satisfaction. He knew that he would have to convince himself that such a thing were possible before he could make his case in print. With an almost fanatical zeal he researched the period and subjected every detail from his patient's testimony to the scrutiny of two acknowledged authorities on the period, Professor René Nelli and Jean Duvernoy. After years of meticulous investigation they concluded that the testimony was in essence and in substance absolutely and unquestionably historically accurate.

## Reading the Akashik Records

German-born psychic healer Karin Page describes what she sees and senses when reading a client's Akashik Records, a fanciful term for the universal matrix of mental energy Jung called the collective unconscious.

> I begin by looking into their aura, the radiance of etheric energy surrounding the body. Often I will see scenes from their former lives as vivid impressions as if I was sharing their memories, or a guide may appear and lead me into a flashback from their former life. Even

*though the features of my client will be different, their personality and physical characteristics will be strikingly similar. Frequently I will see a transfiguration as the face of their former self is superimposed on their present features. It is nearly always a significant scene, rarely a mundane or routine incident and even if its significance is lost to me the client will say, 'now I understand why such and such has been happening to me', or, 'that explains why I have had a lifelong fear of something'.*

Karin has also experienced the benefits of regression for herself.

*I used to suffer from intense migraines until a regression session revealed the source of my headaches. I learnt that I had a life in Scandinavia as the young wife of an uncouth publican in which my only pleasure had been horse riding. Under hypnosis I saw myself riding this beautiful white horse and felt the exhilaration and freedom that I had enjoyed at that time. Then the horse shied and I fell, striking my head on one of the kegs of ale in the yard and died from a fatal head injury. After that session I never suffered from migraines again.*

*Regression has also helped me to discover my karmic connection to other people and why I feel the need to look out for them in this life. I have even learnt why I have a compulsion to keep a full larder of food. It appears that I had a life as an impoverished Indian girl who was hanged by a mob for stealing food for her seven starving brothers and sisters. Curiously, when I was born in my present incarnation the umbilical cord wrapped itself around my neck and I was suffocated. The doctors managed to revive me, but for years afterwards I had this strangulation scar around my neck.*

Sceptics might argue that such 'recollections' are merely symbolic distortions of a traumatic birth, but such theories do not explain other more extraordinary coincidences.

Karin recalls a time when she was regressed to a life as a novice monk in medieval Cologne.

*I died in a fire and witnessed the abbot's vain attempt to rescue me. I immediately recognised him as someone I*

113

*knew in my present incarnation and later learnt that my friend had been told independently by a clairvoyant that he had a former life as an abbot in Cologne. It was the confirmation I needed, although when you re-experience a past life you know intuitively at the core of your being if it is true or not. I don't need a scientist's approval to convince me of the validity of my experience.*

Perhaps the most extraordinary past-life story concerned Karin's connection with celebrated psychic surgeon Stephen Turoff. Turoff claims his miraculous healing powers are due to his disembodied guide Dr Kahn who was a renowned surgeon in nineteenth-century Vienna.

*I went to Stephen for treatment many years ago. He was then working in trance. He allowed Dr Kahn to possess his body, guide his hands and speak through him. The physical transformation from the gentle six-foot giant to wizened physician was striking. Through Stephen, Dr Kahn told me that he had been looking after me since I was a child and that I would understand the significance of what he said very soon. I later learnt during meditation of a former life in Vienna as the wife of a poor medical student who had tried to deliver our baby at home by himself. But I died in childbirth and as I died I saw him on his knees weeping and vowing to become the best doctor in all Europe so that no mother would have to die in childbirth as I had done. He [my husband, the student] had been the son of Dr Kahn and our baby returned to me in my present life as my son. So I learnt that nothing and no one is really lost to us. Separation and grief are only temporary. Our love ensures that we meet again.*

# A past-life regression

Aurora, a 47-year-old care worker living in the UK, had always suspected that she and her husband had shared a series of lives, but it was only after she assented to psychic regression that she had the confirmation she needed.

*My husband and I share an uncommon understanding which is more than mere compatibility. But I wanted to know the details so I consulted a clairvoyant who had been recommended by a friend. It was important for me to find someone with integrity that I could trust as this was something sacred to me, not something that I was doing out of idle curiosity.*

Aurora was regressed by a clairvoyant who shared her client's visions.

*That was the extraordinary aspect. She saw what I saw. She wasn't leading me like a hypnotist, but was describing things in the scene that I hadn't mentioned as if she was standing beside me. She wasn't simply taking my lead.*

*I immediately recognised and identified with each of the personalities she described. It was like opening a book and revealing the divine meaning behind all that had happened to me. All my lives had been for a purpose and now I know how I became the person that I am today.*

*But even though my husband is my soul mate, that didn't mean that every life we shared was a happy one. In one life he was a lord and much older than me. I loved another man but was forced to marry the lord against my will. It ended violently for us all.*

The clairvoyant who regressed Aurora offers to paint pictures of her clients as they appeared in their former lives. Aurora observes:

*There is some of me in all of them. Whether she depicted me as a man or a woman there was something I recognised in the eyes. No wonder they say that the eyes are the windows of our soul.*

*Regression made me realise that you cannot be a complete person unless you can face your darker side. But even our darkest lives have a purpose. During one regression session I discovered I had been a sailor in the early eighteenth century and was mean to the marrow because I had suffered violence and abuse in childhood so I had a grudge against the world. It's not an excuse, but it explains that circumstances can determine your character and influence your actions even if your soul is pure. It also helped explain the source of recurrent chest pains which I had been suffering periodically for several years. Victor, the sailor, had been stabbed in the chest*

115

*and these pains were physical symptoms of a wound that went deeper than the physical. It was effectively nagging me to acknowledge that aspect of myself and not deny it. Once I did so, the pain went. Revealing such unpleasant facts about yourself teaches you not to judge other people so readily and not to be too hard on yourself either. You can be told to be more tolerant and compassionate, but it will have no real effect until you experience what it feels like to be on the dark side.*

## False memories

If memory is a purely physical function of the brain, as the scientists believe, how is it possible to recall impressions from a past life?

Until we can answer this basic question the case for past-life regression cannot be proven conclusively and the evidence for and against is confused by conflicting theories. Fortunately, the laws of the universe do not require the endorsement of science before they can operate.

For the moment all we know for certain is that we possess both a short- and a long-term memory and that while the former is transient and capable of being interrupted, the latter causes a permanent physical change in brain tissue by affecting the growth of nerve cells called micro-neurones. Long-term memory patterns have been proven to last for up to 100 years and are capable of surviving shocks, anaesthetics and even freezing.

It is even possible to recover a memory of which the subject is not aware by electronically stimulating a specific part of the brain. This phenomenon was discovered in the 1960s by Dr Wilder Penfield, an American neurologist who was able to operate on patients while they were still conscious as there are no pain receptors in the brain. None of the recovered impressions originated in his patient's past lives because the brain can only store stimuli that it has processed, while past-life memories are imprinted on the unconscious, which is the immortal, non-physical essence of our being.

This ability of the brain to store sensory impressions which the individual is not consciously aware of is called 'cryptomnesia' and is often cited as evidence in the case against reincarnation. The argument runs that it is impossible to know for certain if a past-life memory is genuine or if it is confused with a forgotten incident in the present lifetime.

But whilst you should always be aware that your past-life memories could be unconsciously sourced from something more mundane, cryptomnesia does not explain how it is possible for some people, while under hypnosis, to speak in a language they have never learnt (a phenomenon known as 'xenoglossia') or exhibit talents which they had not studied or developed in their present life.

The case of Bridey Murphy, arguably the most celebrated example of past-life regression on record, lost considerable credibility when it became known that housewife Virginia Tighe had been raised by an Irish nanny from whom, it was argued, she might have picked up crucial facts about the period and certain parochial expressions. But whilst it is possible to have acquired key phrases and expressions in early childhood and to have forgotten these later in life, it is not possible to speak fluently in an archaic tongue unless you have studied it and such conscious experiences cannot, of course, be dismissed by citing cryptomnesia's 'hidden memory' theory.

The other tendency to be aware of is 'paramnesia', or 'false memory syndrome'. This can arise out of the subject's unconscious desire to please their therapist. It is a form of fantasy in which the subject identifies with something which has not been a part of their personal experience and can be symbolic of an issue which does need to be addressed. It is easily identifiable by the fact that the images can be manipulated and altered at will, as with figments of the imagination.

# Hypnotism and the power of suggestion

Even the most fervent believers in past-life regression will grudgingly admit that hypnotism is not the most reliable method for gathering evidence. During a trance subjects are not only open to suggestion from the therapist, but can also fall victim to self-deception. Detractors often cite a series of case studies conducted in the 1960s by the Finnish psychiatrist Dr Reima Kampman which appear to discredit all alleged recollections of past lives obtained under hypnosis. But while Dr Kampman's experiments reveal that subjects can unwittingly adopt another person's history as their own, they also confirm that we have the capacity to recall even the most seemingly insignificant incidents buried deep in our unconscious. And if that is indeed true it strengthens, not weakens, the arguments in favour of past-life regression.

Kampman recruited volunteers from among the most academically gifted pupils in Finland's secondary schools, among them a 15-year-old girl who recalled a previous life as a boy. Under hypnosis the girl was able to supply the boy's name, his father's name (Aitmatov) and also his occupation (ship's captain). But the most convincing testimony was her description of the boy's lonely life, his feelings for his father and the details of his death by drowning in Lake Issykjokul. After she had returned to waking consciousness the girl remembered nothing of her former life. It appeared to be the most convincing case of past-life recall recorded to date.

It was only after Dr Kampman regressed the girl on a subsequent occasion and asked her where she had first heard of the boy and his father that the truth was revealed. It transpired that many years earlier she had read a novel called *The White Ship* which was set around Lake Issykjokul and featured a lonely little boy who drowned himself in similar circumstances. The author's name was Aitmatov.

Dr Kampman concluded that in this case his subject had unconsciously adopted a secondary personality. Although she could not remember having read the stories on which these fantasies were based she had evidently absorbed them on both an intellectual and an emotional level and had convinced herself that she had lived the life she had only read about.

An even more extraordinary example was that of a 19-year-old girl who gave elaborate details of her life as an English innkeeper's daughter during the thirteenth century. To Kampman's astonishment, while under hypnosis she began to sing a popular song of the period. Again, she had no recollection of her previous life or of the song after being brought back to waking consciousness. Subsequent research identified the song and confirmed that the language she had sung it in was indeed medieval English. It was only when Dr Kampman regressed her a second time and asked her where she had first heard the song that the girl recalled the day she had glanced through a book on the history of music by composer Benjamin Britten and Imogen Holst. From the description Kampman was able to locate the book and confirm that the song was included, rendered in a simplified form of medieval English which his subject had never studied and could only have seen for a few moments all those years ago.

# Reincarnation – FAQs

During my meditation and psychic development workshops I am often asked the same dozen or so core questions concerning past lives and reincarnation. This may be the most appropriate point to raise these issues and clear up some popular misconceptions.

## *Why is it necessary to reincarnate?*

It is only by experiencing the full variety of life on earth and interacting with each other that we can evolve as individuals and collectively as a species. In seeing ourselves the way others see us we come to know our true nature and become aware of our potential. While we are in the realm of spirit, between lives, we cannot influence the course of life on earth. By taking on a physical form we can hope to shape the world in the likeness of the heavenly paradise from which we have come.

## What happens to the soul if there is a miscarriage or abortion or the child dies while very young?

The soul simply returns to the higher realm and awaits another opportunity to reincarnate. Frequently the soul will return to the same parents if they are successful in giving birth to another child and it may retain a memory of the short life it led if it died very young. There have been cases of children born after the death of a sibling describing the life of the other child as if it had been their own.

It is thought that while the embryo is in the womb the incoming soul is not fully integrated and does not commit itself to life until it takes its first breath after birth. Miscarriages may have a purely physical cause but there is also the possibility that the incoming soul decided that the time was not right for it to incarnate.

## Can I choose the circumstances of my next incarnation?

Yes. Your level of spiritual development determines your next incarnation because only you can decide what lessons and experience you will need from the next life and which people you will need to meet in order to resolve your karmic debts. Your higher self knows the difference between what you want and what you need in order to grow and realise your potential. It knows what you have experienced in former lives and what remains to be experienced, cleared and understood. If you were able to determine the circumstances of your next life now you would no doubt make a comfortable life for yourself, but unfortunately we do not learn from an easy life. You might choose to have a life in which all your wishes are gratified, but the only lesson you are likely to learn from such a life is that possessions do not bring happiness.

## Will I always be the same sex?

The evidence suggests that we experience both male and female incarnations, though we may have an unbroken series of lives as one sex. The soul transcends gender, which is a purely physical aspect of nature, but it needs to integrate what we consider to be male and female characteristics if it is to become a fully realised being.

## Is it safe to explore past lives with children?

No, because children are not sufficiently grounded and can easily be disturbed by images which may surface during regression or visualisation exercises. They are not always able to determine what is real and what is imagined and may be unable to process certain feelings and images because of their limited experience and understanding. Regression could instil fear into a child which they might not be able to articulate or put into a context which they can deal with. But often a child will volunteer information about a former life in a casual manner and this should be accepted as naturally as it is offered. It is fine to gently probe for more information to determine whether the story was fact or fantasy, but the child should not be made to feel that the subject is unusual or they may begin to feed you what they think you want to hear, invalidating any genuine memories they may have had.

## Do I have to reincarnate at least once in every culture and country in the world?

There is no universal law that states that you have to experience every form of life or live in every country on earth. You determine what experiences you need and these are likely to involve a diverse series of lives among people of different races, religions and cultures.

## How many years will I have to wait between lives?

Again, this is determined by what you need. If you have lived a long and demanding life you may need more time to recover and assimilate your experiences than if you died young and need to finish what you had started. Those who die in infancy can choose to return within a few years, frequently to the same parents, whereas adults may need the same number of years between lives as they had on earth. If life is cyclical, as the Eastern philosophies believe, it would be logical if the time spent between lives was comparable to the number of years endured on earth.

## What if I discover that I have done something terrible in a former life?

There is no reason to feel guilty for doing something of which you have no conscious knowledge and for which there is no proof that you were personally involved. In all probability everyone on earth has done something bad at one time or another, in this life or in the last. The consequences of these actions are covered by karma, the universal law of cause and effect, which seeks to restore balance. There is no element of judgement or punishment involved, but instead we are presented with opportunities to make amends for any wrong we may have caused. So long as you do no harm to others and act according to your conscience in your present incarnation, then you will have nothing to reproach yourself for.

## Will I feel physical pain or become emotional if I revisit a violent or disturbing incident from a former life?

Usually you are a detached observer of your former self while in a state of hypnotic regression, but in very rare instances you may relive the crucial moment in order to clear a memory or emotional blockage caused by your suppression of that memory. In such cases an experienced professional regression therapist will be able to guide you through the experience without any lasting ill-effects.

## What happens if I see my own death?

Again, in most cases you will be an emotionally detached observer of the scene. The strongest emotion you are likely to feel is intense curiosity. But if there is an emotional disturbance you should surrender to it, as it obviously needs to be cleared.

## What should I do if I discover during regression that I have a soul mate. Should I leave my partner?

Assuming that you have chosen your present partner because there is an emotional bond between the two of you and assuming too that you are not deeply unhappy, you cannot make or break relationships on the advice of a psychic or regression therapist. Only you can decide if the relationship is worth committing yourself to, or not.

The popular misconception is that a soul mate is your perfect partner and that without them you are somehow incomplete. In truth it is often a disaster for soul mates to be lovers as they are too alike and are unlikely to have a productive relationship. The ideal partner is someone you find compatible but not perfect so that you can grow together in the give and take of a real relationship.

## What happens between lives and will I remember this too?

The belief in a heavenly paradise is common to all cultures, ancient and modern, presumably because there is some basis in fact for such beliefs. Contemporary descriptions of the heavenly state given by people who have had a near-death experience are remarkably consistent in substance and in detail, despite the fact that these individuals come from contrasting cultures, backgrounds and beliefs. They describe leaving their body, being drawn through a tunnel of light to emerge in a pastoral paradise where the colours are more vivid than those on earth and the sense of serenity is so pervasive that they are reluctant to return. Such stories might seem too good to be true, but perhaps if you think of it not as a place but as a state of being then it might seem less fanciful. For this reason you are unlikely to recall anything of the state between lives.

## Could I reincarnate on another planet?

There are people who claim to have 'channelled' information from extraterrestrials and higher discarnate life forms, offering confirmation of humanoid life in other solar systems, but channelling is a very questionable activity. Very little of any consequence has been received through channellers other than vague apocalyptic warnings and sermons on why we should all be nice to each other, which suggests that the source of such homilies is far closer to home. There are people who believe that they have memories of previous lives on other planets, but again, their descriptions seem fanciful and idealised in the extreme. The suspicion is that such visions are a form of wish-fulfilment which brings the individual the attention they seem to be seeking.

Of course there may well be life on other planets, but even if that is the case the chances are that it will not be in any form we recognise and we would be unlikely to recall them in terms which are suspiciously close to science fiction clichés.

## Do animals reincarnate and is it possible I might be an animal in my next life?

All higher forms of animal life demonstrate intelligence to varying degrees, which makes it likely that they possess a soul and so could, in theory, reincarnate. But instinct and intelligence are not the same as consciousness, which involves a degree of self-awareness that animals do not possess, meaning that they would not have the free will to choose to reincarnate. Nor would there be any purpose in their doing so if they were not able to exercise free will.

If you experience life as an animal during regression it is likely to be symbolic of your connection with the animal aspect of your psyche (i.e. your cunning, curiosity, mobility, vitality, social needs and instincts). It is possible that we may possess these characteristics because we once had a life in animal form, as it might be necessary for us to pass through the various levels in order to evolve, but once we have become a conscious human being we cannot regress down the evolutionary chain.

Buddhists believe that it is possible for a human being to reincarnate as an animal, but it would be unnatural for a human mind to occupy a lower form of life and it would be against the universal law of evolution.

# 2

# Awareness Exercises

Note: the exercises in this book are intended for relaxation and increasing self-awareness. However, if you have recently experienced mental or emotional problems or are taking medication you should seek professional medical advice before practising meditation on your own. The author and publisher accept no responsibility for any harm caused by or to anyone as a result of the misuse of these awareness exercises.

*Believe nothing which depends only on the authority of your masters and priests. After investigation, believe that which you have yourselves tested and found reasonable and which is for your good and that of others.*
(Buddha, *Kalama Sutta*)

## A note on the awareness exercises

Despite the wealth of experiential evidence on offer it can be difficult to accept the existence of the dream body and related phenomena unless you have personally experienced these heightened states of awareness. The following exercises offer you the opportunity to attain these altered states at will in safe incremental steps beginning with basic meditation and visualisation techniques, expanding awareness to sense and see the aura, or etheric energy field, and culminating with basic mediumship and an exercise designed to induce an out-of-body experience. It is not possible, nor would it be desirable, to induce a near-death experience, but if you are patient and practise these exercises on a regular basis you will develop your natural latent capacity to expand your awareness beyond the physical dimension and explore the inner and upper worlds at will.

# Establishing the habit

The first and arguably most difficult stage is establishing the habit of sitting still, in silent meditation. In the West we have been conditioned to believe that relaxation is unproductive and indulgent, but the opposite is true. We owe it to ourselves to take time out and cultivate a sacred space in which to attain peace of mind and a sense of well-being. As someone once said, if you do not take time for meditation now you will have plenty of time for reflecting on a wasted life and for illness later on.

Initially you are likely to meet inner resistance, as the ego, or inner child as it is sometimes called, reminds you of all the pleasant things you could be doing instead of sitting still, while your inner parent will nag you about the chores that need doing and try to persuade you that meditation has no real value. Learn to ignore them both and you will find that you become more efficient and easier to live with, and in time meditation will become pleasantly addictive. Both chattering voices will recede allowing the voice of your higher or true self to finally be heard. Then you will be receptive to guidance that will be of more value than any that might be given to you by an earthly guru.

The second step is to establish a regular routine rather than waiting for a convenient moment because there will always be something that seems to need doing more urgently than the meditation. Ten to twenty minutes a day, twice a day, first thing in the morning and last thing at night is all you will ever need to solve your most perplexing problems, shrug off any unpleasantness from the day and heal your mind, body and spirit. Do not be tempted to increase it though, as you risk becoming a 'bliss junkie'.

Keep your feet on the ground and your sense of perspective by grounding yourself and closing down after each session. This can be done simply by going for a short walk, taking a shower, drinking a glass of water, thinking about what you plan to do with the rest of the day or simply stamping your feet to re-establish contact with the physical world. Grounding and closing down is particularly important if you practise mediumship as you do not want to remain receptive to discarnate souls 24 hours day, nor do you want to be psychologically unbalanced by failing to assimilate the energy and impressions that are attained through altered states of consciousness.

# Creating the right atmosphere

You can encourage yourself to meditate by creating a tranquil atmosphere and a sense of sacred space with candles, crystals, incense, fresh flowers and appropriate ornaments such as statues of Buddha, inspirational pictures or angels. In time this area will become 'charged' with your positive mental energy and a sense of peace making it an ideal place for quiet contemplation.

Not everyone responds to sitting in silent reflection for long periods of time so consider the use of a cassette or CD player, as appropriate music, recorded visualisations and natural sounds can be very helpful in creating a conducive atmosphere.

Whatever room you dedicate to meditation you will need to ensure your peace and privacy. If there are other people in the house or flat let them know in advance that this is to be a time when you are not to be disturbed and put a note to that effect on the door. Finally, before each session take the phone off the hook or switch on the answering machine.

Note: it is perfectly normal to feel apprehensive at times when you begin a programme of self-realisation, so if you feel uncomfortable at any time during an exercise all you have to do is count down slowly from ten to one and open your eyes. Usually the anxiety has gone before you get to one and so you can resume the meditation.

# Exercise 1: Quietening the mind

Unless you are fortunate to have had an involuntary OBE, the only way you can experience altered states of awareness is to open what is known as the third eye, the organ of psychic sight. And the first step in preparing yourself for this development is passive meditation, which enables you to still the restless chatter of the conscious mind. It is not as simple as it sounds, but it is vital if you want to develop psychic sensitivity and trigger out-of-body experiences at will.

Make yourself comfortable, close your eyes and focus on your breath. Establish a relaxed, regular rhythm and as you do so feel the tension being expelled from your body. If intrusive thoughts arise don't try to suppress them but let them pass and immerse yourself in silence.

Let go and allow yourself to sink into a state of deep relaxation.

When you are fully relaxed and your mind is still, visualise a white circle against a black background. See how long you can sustain this image. When you can maintain it for a few minutes without being distracted or feeling the need to fidget, visualise it being drawn towards you. As it grows larger you can see that it is a radiant white light which intensifies as it draws closer. But it is not blinding to your inner eye. It fills the room and now you can step into it. What do you see on the other side?

When you are ready, open your eyes and return to a state of waking consciousness.

Note: at some point in this series of exercises you may see a single eye looking back at you. It can be quite unsettling, but do not let it disturb you. It signals the opening of your own inner eye, the eye of your higher self.

# Exercise 2 : Projecting awareness

Make yourself comfortable, close your eyes and focus on the breath until you are in a state of deep relaxation.

Now begin to visualise your surroundings in as much detail as you can. Some people find visualisation particularly difficult, so be patient. It will come in time. If you need to, open your eyes from time to time and fix the image of the room in your mind.

When this image is reasonably stable visualise walking very slowly around the room and occasionally looking back at yourself sitting in the chair. Try to sustain this third-person perspective for as long as you can before returning to waking consciousness.

You can develop this visualisation by imagining going out of the front door and taking a walk around the neighbourhood. Use your five senses as much as you can to make the experience real.

Note: this is not daydreaming. Imagination is the means by which we develop the ability to project the mind beyond the confines of the physical body. In time, you may find that even if you lack the confidence to leave your body during the exercise you may begin to trigger involuntary OBEs during sleep.

# Exercise 3: Sensing the aura

If you have ever sensed that someone near you was in a bad mood, or felt that your personal space has been invaded when a stranger sat next to you on the train, then you may be sensitive to the aura – the etheric energy field which emanates from every living creature, even plants. The aura is believed to have seven layers, each one emanating from a specific energy centre in the etheric body; these energy centres are commonly known as 'chakras' from the Hindu word meaning 'wheel'.

With practice you can develop the ability to see the various layers, which will enable you to 'read' the physical, emotional, mental and spiritual state of friends and family members and diagnose any disorders before the physical symptoms appear.

But initially it will be sufficient to tune in to the subtle energy emanating from your own body because once you can feel the etheric field that surrounds you it should be easier for you to accept the existence of the etheric body, which is undetectable to the five physical senses.

Place your hands together, palms inward, until they are almost touching. Then repeatedly pull them apart, to leave a gap of an inch or so, and bring them together again as if you were clapping but without making contact. Within a few minutes you should feel the resistance building up as if you were squeezing a balloon between your hands.

To see the aura all you have to do is place one hand at arms length against a plain white background, such as a wall or table top, with the fingers splayed, then soften your gaze to look past your hand to the background so that your hand is out of focus.

You should begin to see a thin electric blue radiance around your fingers. This is the first layer of the aura. In time you should be able to see it surrounding other people and it can occur spontaneously whenever you are in a deeply relaxed state.

With the development of Kirlian electrophotography, Russian scientists appear to have proven the existence of the aura surrounding all living things that psychics have been able to see unaided for centuries. Science has dubbed this radiance the 'bioplasmic' or 'energy' body and observed that the quality and colour of the aura emitted by a human being corresponds to their health and state of mind, a conclusion that the Greek philosopher Plutarch arrived at nearly 2000 years ago.

## Exercise 4: Inducing an OBE

This exercise will enable you to leave your physical body at will and explore the astral dimension in your dream body.

You might find it conducive to dim the electric lights and light an incense burner or scented candle. But if you use candles, ensure they are secure and preferably standing in a bowl with a few centimetres of water. The use of candles, incense or recordings of music or natural sounds can also help trigger subsequent episodes, as your unconscious will associate the sound or scent with a specific state of mind.

When you have created a suitable atmosphere, lie flat on your back on your bed, sofa or exercise mat with your arms loosely by your sides and your head supported by a pillow. Keep your legs straight.

Establish a regular steady rhythm of breathing and as you sink deeper into relaxation, sense a warming of the solar plexus centre or chakra beneath your navel. Imagine a soft pulsing light in your abdomen as this energy centre, the seat of the emotions, softens, freeing the silver cord that connects the dream body to your physical shell. Feel your body becoming lighter with every breath as you begin to lose awareness of the weight and solidity of your body. With each exhalation visualise a cushion of air forming under you until you feel that you can float away on this cloud.

127

Now feel yourself rising a few inches and then returning as you enjoy exercising control over what is usually a spontaneous experience.

Remember that you are in control at all times and can return to your body at will.

The first few times that you experiment with projecting consciousness in this way it is advisable to explore your immediate environment until you have built sufficient confidence to venture further.

When you are out of the body, look back and observe as much detail as you can. What are your feelings? What attitude do you have towards the body on the bed? Examine your hands and look at yourself in a mirror if you have one. Try to touch everyday objects.

Remember: you are under no obligation to try this exercise. Out-of-body experiences are a natural phenomenon and should never be forced. If you feel uncomfortable for any reason do not attempt this exercise or you risk instilling fear in yourself, which may inhibit your development.

## Exercise 5: The astral visit

The object of the exercise is to obtain conclusive proof of your ability to travel to another location at will in your dream body.

To obtain a truly objective result in this experiment you will need the co-operation of a friend whom you can trust and whose home you are familiar with. Ask your friend to put a book of their choice on a chair in their bedroom with the cover face up. They must not tell you which book they are going to place there and they should not choose one until that evening, otherwise it is possible that you will obtain the answer by telepathy instead.

Then decide on a specific time for the experiment so that they can note any changes that occur in the atmosphere and can be alert at the time you have agreed.

It is vital that your friend is sympathetic to the idea and will take it seriously otherwise you risk having your own confidence undermined. Again, be patient. It may take several nights to make the breakthrough.

## Exercise 6: Project yourself into tomorrow

You can experiment with your innate ability to project your essential self to another location by following these simple steps.

Sit in a comfortable chair and allow yourself to sink gradually into a state of deep relaxation.

Now visualise a white dot pulsating in the centre of your forehead. Sense it as a soft, warm glow that grows with every breath. See it expanding until it covers your face and then imagine a scene coming into focus in that space like a view through an open window.

The scene should be in a location that you intend to visit tomorrow. It could be the home of a friend or family member, a workplace or your school; anywhere that you are not expected to be at this moment but somewhere you can visit tomorrow to confirm if the people at that location saw you today.

While you are visualising yourself visiting this place try to do something unusual so that you will be asked about it when you visit in person. Then you can be sure that your experiment was successful.

Rehearse your journey and visit in as much detail as you can, paying special attention to the sensory aspects: touch, taste, smell and sound.

## Exercise 7: Project yourself into the past

You are now ready to experience your first past-life regression session. This exercise can be performed lying down or seated, but if you are lying on a bed or mat remember to support your head with a pillow.

During a regression there is no need to be anxious. You are in control at all times. If you feel uneasy for any reason simply return to waking consciousness by counting down from ten to one.

Make yourself comfortable, close your eyes and focus on your breath. With every inhalation repeat the phrase 'calm and centred' and with every exhalation repeat the phrase 'deeply relaxed'.

Let your mind settle and your thoughts subside. Do not try to induce an experience. Simply let go and allow yourself to sink into a state of deep relaxation and profound peace as if you were settling into a warm scented bath.

When you feel suitably relaxed, visualise yourself enveloped in a white mist. It is so dense that you cannot see beyond it. Looking down all you can see are your feet at the top of a flight of steps. The mist clears just enough to reveal that you are standing at the top of a spiral staircase. The lower steps are obscured by the mist. Steady yourself by gripping the handrail to your right and count aloud as you descend.

'One ... I am relaxed and ready ... two ... going down ... three ... deeper ... four ... deeper ... five ... down and round ... six ... going deeper ... seven ... deeper down ... eight ... relaxed and ready ... nine ... deeper ... ten ... down.'

You have reached the bottom of the staircase, but still all you can see are your feet and the ground. What type of footwear, if any, are you wearing? What kind of ground are you standing on? The mist begins to clear. You are outside in a landscape that is strangely familiar. Do you recognise this place? Can you tell which country it is from the scenery or the plants? What is the season? Are there any clues as to what period you might be in? What feelings do you associate with this place?

Feel free to explore, knowing that you can return to waking awareness whenever you choose.

Are there any buildings nearby? If so, are you attracted to one in particular? Approach the entrance. Did you live here? Did you work here? If not, what did you do here? Who were your neighbours and what is your abiding memory of this place?

Go inside and look around. Have no fear. No one can harm you. You have returned because there is something of significance for you here. What is it?

Is there a mirror or a basin of water in which you can see your reflection? What clues can you find to your identity? Is it a period from which there might be photographs, or a portrait?

If this is a place you knew in a former life you should know what is around the next corner. Test your memory by trying to find specific rooms.

Perhaps there is a skill that you used to practise in a particular room, or a device that you operated? If so, can you locate it and remember how it works?

Perhaps you were a person of importance and this place might hold a clue as to why you feel that you are under-appreciated in your present life? Or perhaps something bad happened here and you left this life bearing resentment towards someone or guilt for something that you did. If so, do not indulge in these dead emotions. Return with the details, so that you can address the issue at a later date, but leave the emotions behind. If there is a basin of water nearby, plunge your hands into it and let the residue of your emotional energy dissolve in the water. If not, clutch an object and discharge the negative energy into this.

When you are ready, return to waking consciousness in the usual way and ensure that you ground yourself. It might be useful to keep a journal of your impressions from these sessions so that you do not forget anything of significance, and you may see a connection or pattern if you have various accounts for comparison.

# Exercise 8: Inducing a lucid dream

Just before you are ready to go to sleep affirm in words of your own choosing that you are going to enter a state of deep, restful, revitalising sleep and that at a specific point you are going to become aware that you are dreaming. This realisation will be triggered by the sight of a predetermined symbol or object. It should be something that would be incongruous in most dream scenes, such as a giant blue apple, or something more direct, such as a sign saying 'You are dreaming'.

Then as you settle down to sleep, visualise yourself exploring a peaceful dreamlike environment such as a garden or a house of which you have pleasant memories. See the symbol you have chosen and behind it an open door, which you step through into a radiant light. Do not be tempted to imagine anything beyond this so that you do not influence the imagery you will see when you explore the inner landscape for real.

It is unlikely that you will be successful on your first attempt, so be patient and persistent.

## Exercise 9: How to see a ghost

Although discarnate spirits are all around us, most of us are insensible to their presence as we need to be grounded in the material world in order to function and focus on our daily lives and responsibilities without undue distractions. However, we all have the capacity to become attuned to the residual personal energy that acutely sensitive individuals can perceive when they 'open up' to the subtle influences surrounding us. As the Russian mystic Ouspensky observed, certain locations remain charged with the thoughts, feelings, moods and memories of their previous inhabitants.

If you live in an old house you can tune in to the residual impressions of the previous residents using the following exercise. Otherwise you will need to find a suitable place such as an old church or hospital where you can sit for an hour or so in comparative peace.

✦ Keeping your eyes open, still the mind by focusing on your breath. Let your thoughts subside so that you settle into a passive state, receptive to the subtle impressions around you.

✦ Begin by making physical contact with the place. Stand with your back to a wall and take several deep breaths. If you are a natural medium you might be able to sense or see something straight away. If not, put your hands on something that will have absorbed an impression, such as a chair or church pew. And sit quietly. You may feel cold, heat or a tingling in your fingers. The atmosphere may also change in a subtle but significant way as you become sensitised.

✦ Next, heighten your sense of smell. If you are outside expand your awareness by centring on the scent of the grass, flowers and the soil. Hospitals will have their own distinct smells, and churches too will have retained the smell of incense, flowers and polished wood.

✦ Now raise your awareness to the sounds that surround you and then see if you can go beyond those to the vibrations at the higher frequencies. To do this, listen acutely to your watch or a clock. Home in on the ticking to the exclusion of everything else.

✦ Finally, soften your gaze so that any reflected light, such as through a stained glass window or off a polished surface, has a mildly hypnotic effect. Look beyond the light into the middle distance and see if you can detect a shape or figure. If not, look away into a dark corner and see if you can detect any movement in the shadows.

✦ If you are anxious for any reason you can ask your inner guides or guardian angel to draw near, isolating you from any disturbing influences in the atmosphere. You can help the process by stimulating your third eye. Simply make gentle, circular movements with your index finger in the centre of your forehead until you feel a tickling sensation. You are now open to the more subtle impressions in the atmosphere around you.

Remember to close down and ground yourself when you have finished by counting down slowly from ten to one, stamping your feet and thinking about what you are going to do later on or the next day.

## Exercise 10: Speaking with spirits

It is a popular misconception that spirits are summoned at the request of the medium and because of this many people still believe that spirit communication is wrong because it disturbs the peace of the departed. In fact, the reverse is true. Spirits come only when they have something that they are desperate to impart to the living and they use a medium because most of us are not receptive to direct communication.

For this exercise you will need a photograph of the deceased and, if possible, one of their personal possessions such as a watch or a ring.

Take the photograph in one hand and the memento in the other. Make yourself comfortable, close your eyes and focus on your breath.

Begin by drawing a circle of soft golden light around you to raise your awareness to a higher level and exclude any unwelcome influences.

Now sensitise yourself to the residual vibrations in the personal object by centring your awareness in that hand. You should feel warmth or a tingling sensation. If your psychic awareness is becoming more developed you may even have a vision of the person you want to communicate with.

If not, open your heart centre by imagining a small pulsating sphere of green light growing in intensity as you go into a deeper state of relaxation.

Feel your heart centre softening and envisage the person you want to communicate with emerging from the light.

If that person does not appear you may see your inner guide instead. If so, you can ask it to help you find the person you want to communicate with. Do not be surprised if they appear as they were when they were younger or in an idealised form, as this is a projection of their self-image.

However, you may not receive a visual communication. Instead you might have a sense of that person in the room, or hear their voice in your inner ear. If it is a lady you may have a scent of their perfume. If it is a man who smoked you may become aware of the smell of their favourite tobacco.

When you are ready to return to waking consciousness, close down, clear the aura and ground yourself using the techniques that were previously described.

# Exercise 11: Talking to God

You do not have to wait until you ascend to heaven to talk with God. You have a direct line to the divine 24 hours a day, 7 days a week, because you are a part of what you seek, and heaven, as the enlightened have been telling us for centuries, is within.

There are various techniques for contacting the higher self, the Christ consciousness or the Buddha within. Meditation is one method, but it takes time and many of us do not have the patience to wait upon the blessings of providence. So here are just a few alternative techniques that should yield results within a week. But while you are working through the following exercises be patient and persistent. Striving and struggling may produce results in the material world, but the opposite is true in spiritual work. In spiritual development intense activity is counter-productive. Stillness and receptivity open the channel to the inner teacher.

## a) Automatic Writing

Sit with a note-pad and a pen in your lap, close your eyes and visualise the blank sheet of paper in front of you. Now say the following sentence to yourself and write down whatever comes to your mind in response to it.

'I am open to whatever insights are right for me to receive from (substitute any suitable term for the higher self).'

You may want to ask a question about life and death or the purpose of your own life. Feel free to ask whatever you want, but be prepared for a surprising answer when you finally make the connection.

Wait for a minute, then open your eyes and write down whatever thoughts came to mind. If you receive what appears to be nonsense write it down regardless, as this is part of the clearing and connection process. Do not analyse what you receive or you risk blocking the flow. If you receive an uninterrupted stream of words or images, write them down until they come to a natural conclusion. Otherwise, close your eyes and repeat the sentence.

Do this 22 times each session for 6 days then rest for a day and repeat the process for the next 6 days if necessary. If this technique proves particularly productive then feel free to use it anytime you are looking for guidance or perhaps for the interpretation of a dream. But always give yourself a day's rest if you have practised the exercise for 6 days in a row.

You can be sure you have a genuine connection if you find yourself writing faster than you can think. It will be as if you are taking divine dictation. But be wary of any message that comes through telling you what you should, must, ought, could and have to do, or not do. That is the stern, unforgiving voice of the inner parent, that hypercritical aspect of the self that Freud called the superego. In contrast, the higher self is non-judgemental and its messages are given in unconditional love.

## b) Journaling

Another effective technique for opening communications with the higher self is known as journaling. You can use images from your most vivid dreams or from meditation sessions as triggers in a free association exercise if you suspect that they may hold clues to a past life.

In a variation of the previous exercise all you have to do is hold the diary or journal open at a blank page, then close your eyes and repeat the word or phrase that describes the image you want to use as a prompt. If for example you dreamt of someone you don't know in waking life but who, you sensed, you may have known in a past life, then you could use a phrase that describes that person or the setting in which you saw them as a form of mantra to trigger suppressed memories in your unconscious. After a minute sitting in silence, open your eyes and write down anything that comes spontaneously to mind in response. Then close your eyes again and repeat the process until you have contemplated that phrase or image 22 times in total. In this way you are using a dream image to tease out a genuine past-life memory.

Alternatively, you could stimulate a two-way conversation with your true self by simply choosing a word, such as 'angel', 'heaven' or 'God', that has the potential to draw out more related phrases in a free association exercise. Even your own name can produce startling insights into how you see yourself and the sources of any problems.

## c) Dialoguing

Recollect a character from a meditation session or a significant dream and engage in a written conversation with him or her. Write the first thing that comes into your mind regardless of whether it makes any sense to you at that moment. If you persevere there will be a breakthrough, after which the words will flow from your pen before you can consciously think of them. The resulting 'script' should be extremely revealing.

## d) Clustering

Begin by writing a significant detail from a visualisation or dream in the centre of the page. Then draw a line to one edge of the paper and write the first word or phrase that comes to your mind. Circle it and then draw another line from this second bubble until you have covered the page in encircled clues and insights.

## e) Storytelling

Select a few key words or phrases from your most recent vivid dream and use them to construct a story. Don't think too hard or analyse what you are writing. Simply allow the story to unfold and the characters to speak through you. You may discover that you have voiced subconscious concerns that link a past life to your present situation.

# Conclusion

# The Holographic Universe

As we move into the 21st century, science is having to redefine what it means by reality, as it awakens to the fact that the rules that govern matter and energy in the physical universe do not always apply at the subatomic level. Immutable mechanical laws have given way to a world subject to mathematical probability, meaning that nothing can now be stated with certainty.

The paradox of quantum physics raises the possibility of a multidimensional, holographic universe which may not be as solid as we once thought. It feels solid because our physical body is of the same density as our surroundings, but our world of solid matter is an intricate optical illusion, constructed by the brain, which cannot process information fast enough to see between the particles to the world beyond. The brain is like a supercomputer but we only use a tiny proportion of its processing power. When mind and brain separate in meditation, during the deepest stages of sleep or when consciousness floats free of the physical we are no longer filtering sensory input through the five physical senses but are plugged directly into the mainframe, the ultimate reality. Unfortunately, when we recall these experiences the primitive processing power of our brains cannot compute the enormity of this new reality and so the brain reformats the impressions into something we can relate to.

Once we have glimpsed this greater reality, as the late particle physicist James Jeans observed in 1930, 'the universe begins to look more like a great thought than like a great machine'.

## Is God in heaven?

Few people today believe that God exists in the form envisioned in the Bible, as a white-bearded patriarch sitting in judgement on mankind from his celestial throne in the heavens. An increasing number do not believe in

God at all and their doubt is understandable in this age of seemingly random cruelty and injustice in which self-interest is rewarded with celebrity and wealth, while selflessness is frequently considered to be a sign of weakness or even stupidity.

Those who look to the Eastern philosophies or the Western esoteric tradition subscribe to the belief that there is a benign transcendent intelligence overseeing our evolution even if it does not appear to intervene or even take an active interest in our problems. But by believing in an omnipotent celestial being we delegate responsibility to another, a conveniently invisible being whose existence we cannot prove and therefore to whom we can continue to turn to fix things for us, or to blame for everything that we allow to go wrong. The 'will of God' refers to our innate potential and ability to create the world we want to live in, not the whim of fate.

Many, like myself, believe that God is consciousness, the divine spark within every human being; the universal life force that is both within and without, sustaining and surrounding us like the air we breathe or the water that supports all aquatic life. Evil, on the other hand, is simply the conscious denial of our true nature and a wilful disregard to see it in other people.

We deny God's existence (and by inference the existence of heaven too) because it is self-evident that God does not intervene to prevent human tragedies. But that does not mean that God does not exist. We are both God and his creation, as manifest in the higher self and in finite form and unless we accept our obligation to intervene where we see evil or injustice then we will not be able to fulfil our divine destiny which is to create heaven on earth. Until we accept this responsibility we are condemned to live in the hell of our own making.

*I am God, you are God.*
*The only difference is that I know it and you do not.*
(Sri Satya Sai Baba)

# Our fear of death

Death is not a supernatural mystery, but a process of transformation as natural as the changing seasons or the butterfly emerging from its cocoon. The evidence of regeneration is all around us, yet we refuse to see the parallels with our own life cycle.

In the West we have chosen to make death a taboo subject because we fear to face our own mortality and that of those we love. It is understandable that we should dread losing our friends and family, but we need to accept that the separation is only temporary and that grief is an essential part of the human experience. Bereavement forces us to question our self-centred view of the universe so that we can emerge with a more realistic perspective. It awakens us to the importance of living a full and productive life, gives us the opportunity to reassess what is of true value to us and helps to put our problems into perspective. It does not render us powerless or vulnerable; we only fear that it will. If we can accept that our loved ones are now where they need to be in the great cycle of death and rebirth it will alleviate our sense of loss and allow us to move on, maturing with each new experience, and in doing so we will be assisting our loved ones to do the same.

Instead of mourning we should celebrate the life lived to the full and the release of a soul from physical confinement or suffering. Where a promising life has been unexpectedly cut short or terminated naturally before it could begin, we need to see it as a choice made by the individual soul in order to awaken those around it who would not otherwise have contemplated the mysteries of life and death, or perhaps so that it could return at a more favourable time.

Losing a child in any circumstances is unbearable, but even this anguish can be diminished to a degree if, in time, it can be accepted that nothing is lost, only opportunities. One of the ladies I interviewed for this book told me of the time she miscarried and was overcome by grief so intense that she feared she would be consumed by it. In her anguish she cried out for an answer to whomever was responsible for the order of the universe and a moment later a radiance filled her hospital room. In the midst of this light were two angelic beings, each holding an infant, one male and one female. The lady intuitively knew that one was the child she was grieving for and that it had refused to incarnate without the other, its twin. From that moment on the mother was filled with a renewed appetite for life and the knowledge that she would have a second chance to bring both souls to earth. After she recovered sufficiently she pursued IVF treatment and was told by her doctors that she could expect three children from the three implants if successful, but the mother knew she would be having two. In due course she gave birth to twins, a boy and a girl, whom she immediately recognised as the two souls who had come to her in her most desperate moment.

It is easy for someone who is not consumed by grief to view death with philosophical detachment, but as the Buddha observed we have all been touched by loss and life is suffering (samsara), by which he meant that it is a test of our resolve and resourcefulness, not an ordeal to be endured. The only way to cease from suffering is to alter our perception of what is real and so become consciously aware that it is our material world which is the illusion and not the next. Everything in the physical world is transitory – life, possessions, even the earth's physical features are transformed by climate over time. But the next world is eternal. This physical earth of ours may appear solid, but as science has reluctantly acknowledged, solidity is an illusion. The existence of subatomic levels in which dark matter can pass between atoms suggests that heaven may indeed be within and all around us.

If we can cultivate the view that death is not an end but a process of withdrawal from one reality in order to awaken to another, then we may finally lose our fear of death and with it, our fear of life. The real significance of death is that it is the first step in the process of becoming.

> *For those who doubt, no proof is enough; for those who believe,*
> *no proof is necessary.*

(Anon)

# Bibliography
# and Resources

## Bibliography

Atwater, P.M.H. *Coming back to Life* (Ballantine, 1991)

Barrett, W *Death-Bed Visions* (Methuen, 1926)

Crookall, Robert *The Supreme Adventure* (James Clarke & Co, 1961)

Currie, Ian *Visions of Immortality* (Element, 1998)

Edward, John *One Last Time* (Penguin Putnam, 2000)

Fremantle, R. and Trungpa, C., translators *The Tibetan Book of the Dead* (Shambhala, 1975)

Geddes, Sir Auckland 'A Voice from the Grandstand' (*Scottish Medical Journal*, 1927)

Gerhardie, William *Resurrection* (Macdonald, 1973)

Green, Celia *Out-of-Body Experiences* (Institute of Psychophysical Research, 1995)

Guirdham, Arthur *The Cathars and Reincarnation* (Neville Spearman, 1970)

Halevi, Z'ev Shimon ben *A Kabbalistic Universe* (Gateway, 1988)

Holroyd, S. *Mysteries of the Inner Self* (Aldus, 1978)

Huxley, Aldous *The Doors of Perception* (Vintage, 2004)

Jung, C.G. *Memories, Dreams, Reflections* (Vintage, 1961)

Kraalingen, Elleke van *Beyond the Boundary of Life and Death* (Publisher unknown)

Leland, Kurt *The Unanswered Question* (Hampton Roads, 2002)

MacLaine, Shirley *Out on a Limb* (Bantam, 1984)

Moody, R.A. *The Light Beyond* (Rider, 2005)

Moody, R. A. *Life After Life* (Mockingbird Books, 1975)

Monroe, R.A. *Journeys out of the Body* (Doubleday, 1971)

Morse, Melvin *Closer to the Light* (Ivy Books, 1991)

Muldoon, Sylvan *The Phenomena of Astral Projection* (Rider, 1987)

Muldoon, Sylvan *The Case for Astral Projection* (Aries Press, 1936)

Myers, F.W.H. *Human Personality and its Survival of Bodily Death* (Longmans, Green, 1903)
Osis, K. and Haraldsson, E. *At the Hour of Death* (Hastings House, 1977)
Ouspensky, P. *In Search of the Miraculous* (Harvest, 2001)
Praagh, James Van *Talking to Heaven* (Signet, 1999)
Richelieu, Peter *A Soul's Journey* (Thorsons, 1996)
Rinpoche, Sogyal *The Tibetan Book of Living and Dying* (Rider, 2002)
Ring, Kenneth *Life at Death* (Quill, 1982)
Ring, Kenneth *Lessons from the Light* (Moment Point Press, 2000)
Roland, Paul *Explore your Past Lives* (Godsfield, 2005)
Roland, Paul *Investigating the Unexplained* (Piatkus, 2000)
Roland, Paul *The Complete Kabbalah Course* (Foulsham, 2005)
Wheeler, David R. *Journey to the Other Side* (Grosser and Dunlop, 1976)
Zaleski, Carol *Otherworld Journeys* (Oxford University Press, 1988)
Various Editors, *Mysteries of the Unknown* (Time-Life, 1997)

## Resources

http://www.pastlives.net
http://www.hypnoticworld.co.uk/regression_pastlife
http://www.laughingcherub.com/reincarnation.htm
http://www.crystalinks.com/karmasoulgroups.html
http://www.members.optusnet.com.au/~acceptance/
    UnderstandingSpirituality/Spirituality%20Files/SpiritContents.htm
http://www.aish.com/spirituality/kabbala101
http://www.digital-brilliance.com/kab/faq.htm
http://religiousmovements.lib.virginia.edu/nrms/kabb.html
http://www.gnostic-jesus.com
http://www.machers.com/Default.aspx?tabid=161
http://www.kabbalahsociety.org/
http://iands.org/index.php
http://www.nderf.org/
http://www.near-death.com
http://www.vanpraagh.com
http://www.johnedward.net

## Other sources

'A Soul's Journey' by Peter Richelieu. Reprinted by permission of HarperCollins Publishers Ltd © Peter Richelieu 1972.
Extract on page 72 from an article in 'Anabiosis – The Journal of Near Death Studies' Vol 2 Issue 2, December 1982, published by IANDS, PO Box 502, East Windsor, CT 06028 USA (www.iands.org)

# Index